YOU MAKE ME BRAVE

Warrior Women in this Generation

BETHANY LESCH GRUBB

WESTBOW
PRESS®
A DIVISION OF THOMAS NELSON
& ZONDERVAN

Scripture quotations marked "MSG" are from THE MESSAGE. Copyright © *by Eugene H. Peterson 1993, 1994, 1995, 1996, 2000, 2001, 2002.* Used by permission of NavPress Publishing Group.

Unless otherwise noted, Scripture quotations are taken from the *Holy Bible: New International Version*®. *NIV*®. Copyright © 1973, 1978, 1984 by International Bible Society. Used by permission of Zondervan. All rights reserved.

WestBow Press books may be ordered through booksellers or by contacting:

WestBow Press
A Division of Thomas Nelson & Zondervan
1663 Liberty Drive
Bloomington, IN 47403
www.westbowpress.com
1 (866) 928-1240

ISBN: 978-1-5127-4603-7 (sc)
ISBN: 978-1-5127-4604-4 (hc)
ISBN: 978-1-5127-4602-0 (e)

Library of Congress Control Number: 2016909847

Print information available on the last page.

WestBow Press rev. date: 06/27/2016

There's nothing small or inconsequential about our stories. There is, in fact, nothing bigger. And when we tell the truth about our lives—the broken parts, the secret parts, the beautiful parts—then the gospel comes to life, our actual story about redemption, instead of abstraction and theory and things you learn in Sunday school.

If I could ask you to do just one thing it's this: consider that your own silence may be part of the problem. If you've been sitting quietly, year after year, hoping that someone will finally start speaking a language that makes sense to you, may I suggest that you are that person? If you've been longing to hear a new language of faith, one that rises and falls like a song, may I suggest that you start singing? If you want your community to be marked by radical honesty, by risky, terrifying ultimately redemptive truth-telling, you must start telling your truth first.[1]

Shauna Niequist, from *Bittersweet*

CONTENTS

Introduction ix

Part I: The Tension We Experience as Women 1

Chapter 1:   Facing the Darkness 3
Chapter 2:   Head Over Heels 13
Chapter 3:   Embracing Our Differences 23

Part II: The Tension We Experience while Working (as Moms) 37

Chapter 4:   The Demanding "Should Do" List 39
Chapter 5:   Heels and Huggies 52
Chapter 6:   Beautiful Mess 61

Part III: The Tension We Experience as Warriors 65

Chapter 7:   Warrior Women 67
Chapter 8:   Taking Up Arms Together 74
Chapter 9:   Weary Warriors 84
Chapter 10: Eshet Chayil (Women of Valor) 89

Discussion Questions 99
References 103

INTRODUCTION

I initially thought that I would title this book *The Most Unlikely Mother of Five*, because I don't homeschool my children, bake bread, have a garden, or use essential oils. I do have sweet friends who do all of those things, and they seem agonizingly well equipped for the job. I, on the other hand, don't think that I fit the job description. I do not homeschool and never seriously considered the idea. I think that my oldest daughter and I would last one hour in that type of situation. Thankfully, she loves school and her fabulous public school teachers! I don't bake bread, but maybe one day I will. And I dream of one day having a garden. But for now, I can't seem to find the time—and what I planted would probably die anyway.

I grew up with one sister, and my husband grew up with one brother. My husband and I, early in our marriage, talked about having two or three children. When you have three children, one of the ways you get to five is by having twins. Oh, and your husband never quite getting around to having a vasectomy. That (small, in-office surgical procedure) was supposed to happen. My husband and I were sitting together during our first obstetric visit for our fourth pregnancy when my OB was performing an ultrasound and said, "Well, that's going to change things."

"What is?" I asked.

"You have two."

I had entertained the idea of having twins during each of my three previous pregnancies, but this time the thought hadn't even crossed my mind. Wow. I cried, felt overwhelming fear, went into shock, and then cried thankful tears. Could it be that I was going to have twins? I know, Lord, that you do not make mistakes.

God has never made a mistake, and I knew he wasn't making one this time. But I already felt full with life's demands. And God seemed to be beckoning me deeper still. What do you do when you are living with the tension of having to be many women—friend, daughter, manager, mother, lover, leader, counselor, sister, motivator, healer, and helpmate? What do you when you are empowered to lead in certain spheres of life but not others? It was during this season that I began to wrestle with my level of empowerment as a female leader at work, at home, and at church. The lyrics to my favorite song, "You Make Me Brave," kept running through my mind: "For you are for us, you are not against us, Champion of heaven, you made a way for all to enter in." I was longing to hear a language spoken that released us women to be whom the Lord created us to be, his image-bearers, his warriors. We are his warriors.

The tension is real, and it is there. According to *Merriam-Webster*, the word *tension* has two definitions. The first is "the act or action of stretching to tautness," like with a bow and arrow. The second is "inner striving or unrest."[1] Tension can be a good thing, though. An arrow could not soar without tension in the bow.

How do we walk in the tension? We walk in a way that is only made possible through the One who created us to be here. We walk humbly and boldly because we are brave. He makes us brave.

PART 1

The Tension We Experience as Women

Without the full participation of women, we have a world that has one eye covered in trying to see the full picture.

Leymah Gbowee, Nobel Peace Prize winner

Don't, by the way, read too much into the differences here between men and women. Neither man nor woman can go it alone or claim priority. Man was created first, as a beautiful shining reflection of God—that is true. But the head on a woman's body clearly outshines in beauty the head of her "head," her husband. The first woman came from man, true—but ever since then, every man comes from a woman! And since virtually everything comes from God anyway, let's quit going through these "who's first" routines.

1 Corinthians 11:10–12 MSG

CHAPTER 1

Facing the Darkness

I'll never forget the way it felt to walk out the door that day. The morning sun shone so brightly that I was blinded by it. I'd spent the last twelve hours of my life in the Dallas County Jail, not a place people intend to visit. It all felt like a dream, like a crazy, bad dream. I had been married for one year. Many of the rumors you hear are true—about jail, that is, not marriage. In the first two minutes of being there, I remember being struck with the reality that I understood why people never got out, or why it was so difficult to break free from the cycle of crime. In those twelve hours, I was a criminal, subhuman. The guy who'd checked me in and dumped the contents of my purse said, after taking one quick glance, "Well, it looks like you finally got caught. That's what happens with drunks. They get caught."

What? I was thinking. *I just left a pharmaceutical dinner twenty minutes ago and was driving too fast so I could deliver the awesome sushi I had saved for my husband. I knew he was going to love it. I may have some alcoholics in my family, but I'm not the person you just described. I went to Baylor, for goodness' sake. We didn't even have alcohol at our functions.*

I did the official "blow test" and then was put in the holding cell. I sat on the ground with my back against the cold tile wall. It was a diverse group of people in the jail. All I could think was, *How did I get here?* I sat next to the toilet—the steel, rust-ridden, how-long-has-it-been-since-anyone-went-to-the-bathroom-in-that-thing, and is-that-even-legal toilet. I sat with my back against the wall with a full view of the room, which measured ten feet by ten feet. And then the comments started. "Ooh, look at that outfit. Fancy." "Look at those heels. She could take someone out in those heels." I sank back deeper into the wall, wishing I could just disappear. *Am I going to need to take somebody out? Oh my goodness, why am I thinking about taking people out? Isn't this bad enough?* An hour later, a young woman came in and sat next to me. She had a similar story. Well, she had been pulled over in the same spot as I. She was sad about a breakup and had drunk too much at the bar close to her apartment. She said that the police apparently staked out that spot. She was worried about losing her job if she had to tell her boss where she was. A seventeen-year-old who had put graffiti on a building had been brought in. This was her second offense. And then another girl—I think she was sixteen—who was visibly still intoxicated had hit another car while she ran a red light. She was most upset that she wasn't going to receive a McDonald's Egg McMuffin for breakfast in the morning. Because that's how they do things at the fancy jails in Dallas, but not in the big-time jail. You made it to the big time, sister. I mean, *we* made it to the big time.

Those of us who were incarcerated did get one phone call each, and mine was to my husband of one year. It went like this. "Hey," I said in a cracked voice, "I'm okay."

"Where are you?"

"I'm in jail."

"What jail?"

"I think they said Lew Sterrett. I don't know. It's the big one downtown. I thought they were going to let me go or at least let me call you to come get the car. I was just a block away from our apartment."

"I'll come get you."

"Yeah, I think it may take a while."

The phone didn't even look like a phone. There wasn't a receiver that you held up to your ear. There was just a metal square on the wall, and you could only talk as if it were in speaker mode. So people were shouting to be heard.

I almost got into a fight, not during my phone call but when the graffiti girl called home. She was talking to her mom, who basically was saying that she could not pick her up in the morning because she had to go to work. Graffiti girl couldn't hear when her mom told her when she was going to be able to come get her because people were talking loudly.

I said, "Shh," so she could hear. In 0.2 seconds, I had a wiry woman in my face, yelling about how nobody tells her what to do, that I had no idea what she'd been through, and that if I wanted to say anything else to her, I needed to come out with it. I stood my ground and just looked at her as she talked to me. She lowered her voice and kept talking. She told me that her mother was very sick and, since none of her siblings were around to help, that she was the sole caretaker. She had done everything she needed to do for her parole, but her mother was getting sicker, and she had to go check on her. She missed one of her check-ins. She felt defeated because she asked them to give her grace, but they didn't. They brought her in anyway, and she was mad. I got it. Later she thanked me for listening. She said most people wouldn't have done that.

Then all of us in jail that night had to walk into a room and stand before a judge. This was the only time we saw the men who had been brought in.

The judge called your name. Then you stood up and raised your right hand. You vowed that it was really you; you agreed to the charge; and your bail was set. And then you waited.

Everyone in the holding cell got really excited when breakfast came, because it was "good"—two slices of white bread with American cheese in between. This woman loves herself some carbs, and who doesn't love white bread in her heart of hearts? I loved to eat white bread, but not today. I couldn't eat it. I still could not believe that I was there in jail. My error in judgment had landed me there.

The wheels churned slowly, but eventually we inmates were led up to the actual jail cell. I and the now sober sixteen-year-old girl were the first ones to be let out. I thought that her mom should have decided to rethink her decision and let her daughter sweat it out a little longer. Just sayin'. As a mom, I think that a night in jail is a pretty solid natural consequence for a few bad choices. I'm not saying that the mother should have picked her daughter up in a week, but I am saying that she should have let her sweat it out for the day. I'm not opposed to a little tough love. Can I get an amen? I know I felt it—tough love, that is—for my bad choice. The Lord's severe mercy came reaching down.

I am survivor of sexual abuse. I can own it now after twenty years. This part of my story has taken me twenty years to face and has cost me a very high price. I still struggle with anger that unfortunately affects my husband and children most. So I continue to pray and hope for freedom in this area of my life. I see now that the two are related—the sexual abuse (then) and my anger (now). The pain is real when something that I "should have gotten over a long time ago" affects my children.

At sixteen years old, I was sexually abused by someone I trusted, an adult in an organization that I loved. As mentioned above, I didn't begin to have the discussion about my abuse, to face the steel vault over in the corner, until twenty years after it happened. That is a long time to carry the weight of shame and guilt I now know was not mine to own. It took counseling and walking through a curriculum called Shelter from the Storm[1] to put me on the road to healing. It was very interesting to read the lingo and to discover the words, the things we tell ourselves as survivors of sexual abuse. We are masters of minimizing. *It happened a long time ago. I should be over it by now. It wasn't that bad. It wasn't like I was gang raped at knifepoint. People who have experienced those things have a reason to be angry.*

Everybody loved Mindy. I thought she was my best friend. Even after I was abused, I talked about her as if she were my best friend. I locked the abuse away, that part of our relationship. I remember thinking, *She wouldn't do anything to hurt me, right?* Mindy was my leader, my best friend. Her job was to protect me, not to hurt me. Now I see that she is a perpetrator and a predator. She abused me in my room every night for six weeks. It was the summer. She had just finished up a staff position and decided to move to my hometown, "a real hometown," they say. And it was. It was a great place to grow up.

I have worked through many components of the abuse. I identified my coperpetrators (others who did not participate in the abuse but somehow facilitated or did not protect), namely, my parents. What is interesting about this now is that I didn't give them the choice to intercede for me. I see that now. My mom asked me if this person had done anything to make me feel uncomfortable. Right then was the distinct moment I made my choice: it was not worth it to tell the truth.

I have become angry over the years because my family and I did not press charges or take some measure to bring the sexual abuse to light. I felt like my mom just wanted to fix it (or me), so she drove me to a counselor once a week for eight weeks. Fixed. The counselor said that we could press charges, but she also thought I was "going to be okay." I didn't tell because I was concerned about what doing so would look like for my family. One hears a great deal of shame in the stories of sexual abuse survivors. There is the shame that you feel, and the shame that gets mistakenly projected onto you when people ask questions like "Why didn't you stop it?", "How could you let this happen?" and "Why can't you just move on?" I have not been asked those questions, but I know others who have. I think those are the questions that I feared the most.

Add to my scenario the fact that the person who abused me was a woman. A female abuser? Is that even possible? The generational sin of appearance runs deep, and so at sixteen years old I made the decision that my having been abused was mine to own and that the consequences were mine to bear. Alone. In the last few years, my parents and I have dialogued about what happened. My mom said, "I was desperate to protect you, and I failed." Both of my parents have asked for forgiveness, and I have given it. I think that we will have additional conversations. Number one on my list of things to do is to allow the Lord to break that generational sin. It's like peeling an onion; there are more layers underneath. Those who face their abuse, whether physical, emotional, sexual or spiritual are survivors. Survivors are warrior women.

And so, whatever the pain, we make the best decision to simply survive. We keep going. We take on different roles. We do what we have to do to survive. I became the hero. I was not trying to become the hero, but when I read a sheet called "Family Survival Roles," I knew that was me. The hero wants to bring respect to the family name, represses, superachieves, and is desperate to have/prove his or her worth. Um, I still struggle with the last one. Other roles that we can take on after abuse include the scapegoat. The scapegoat is usually blamed for the family's problems, is defiant, is strong, has a harmful peer group, and uses distraction to cope with problems. Another possibility is to become the victim. The victim blames others, has high standards for others, overachieves, is charming, is grandiose, and practices projection and unforgiveness. The surrogate spouse is another role. The surrogate spouse takes the place of the emotionally or physically absent parent and becomes child-counselor for the troubled parent. This individual is usually super-responsible, has physical illnesses, acts like a martyr, practices denial, and is committed to being strong and in control. I think that many of us were able to take on one of these roles in our family of origin if we were subjected to any kind of emotional, physical, verbal, or sexual abuse.

Two things that most helped me to get to the point where I could begin to have the discussion about my abuse were to write a "gut check" at the end of every day for two weeks and to identify what my emotional need may have been so that I allowed myself to be susceptible to a perpetrator's advances. The gut check was a huge eye-opener for me. The guilt, shame, and fear that I felt every single night amounted to a new discovery. I would not have predicted that, so I was surprised when I began to see this pattern emerge. When I felt this way, I wasn't even thinking about my abuse. Instead, I had guilt about not fully engaging with my kids and not finishing the dishes. I had shame that so-and-so was such a good mom because she did crafts with her kids regularly and I'd never do that well. I thought, *I can try, but it is not my gifting.* I had shame over losing my temper and yelling at Sam, my son, for not listening or obeying for the twelve hundredth time. And then I felt fear that I would never be good enough, that my kids would mourn the day and wish they had a better mom, along the lines of, "So-and-so is more fun. She lets her kids do such-and-such. They get to eat blah, blah, blah. I wish I had her for a mom." So identifying guilt, shame, and fear every night for two weeks about things that had nothing to do with my abuse was groundbreaking in that I realized the abuse was still affecting me currently, this day. Yes, it happened twenty years ago, but time does *not* heal wounds. It's better to do some work in order to heal one's wounds.

It felt hard to think about what my emotional need may have been. Why did I have to bear this additional emotional burden when I had done nothing wrong? I wasn't the abuser. Why was I struggling with breaking relationships because a leader I had innocently trusted broke sacred trust with me? My emotional need was that I wanted to feel beautiful and I wanted to be chosen. My younger sister is beautiful. She has blonde hair and blue eyes, and is very sanguine. She got lots of accolades for her appearance. I remember hearing them as a little girl. We were two years apart. While we were standing together in our Easter dresses, I remember hearing, "Oh, you look beautiful. Such a pretty dress. And, oh, that hair! Beautiful. Hi, Bethany." I got the message even at that young age, especially because I heard it many times. My sister is beautiful. Am I not? My sister is also chosen. Am I chosen? In the absence of a boyfriend or a spouse, I looked to my dad for reassurance that I was beautiful and chosen. He seemed to have a natural, easy connection with my sister. Maybe I am harder to love? I was independent. Is that negative? I did not always receive affection. Does that mean I won't be chosen? These are questions I asked myself. My independence, I now understand much better. I even see them in my oldest daughter now. This girl, at eighteen months of age, broke my heart. I came home from my first weekend away, fully expecting a giant hug and maybe a few squeals upon my return. And what did I get? Once I walked in the door, she looked at me, offered no smile, walked the other way, and left the room. Stab. What I have learned about her is that she really did feel as if I had deserted her. She needed time to warm back up to me. I had to work through that as a mom. Sometimes it feels easier to not venture out. When a weekend away with my college besties was a lifeline for me, I had to make a choice. It was good for my heart and for this mama's soul to go, but at the same time I knew that it would take time for my daughter to warm back up to me. At seven, she still doesn't like for me to be gone, but we prepare for it and set expectations.

When I was younger, my physical appearance was always an issue of measuring up. I usually did not measure up. The thing I kept hearing was, "You just need to be ten pounds lighter." This was when I was a 115-pound high schooler who ran cross-country twice a day. Oh my.

My and my parents' biggest throw-down to date was over my weight during college. Having gained the freshman fifteen as a sophomore, I was home and talking with my parents. My mother said, "You're really okay with the way you look? How is that possible?" Stab. I drug my dad (who is a doctor) into the room as the medical voice of reason to validate the fact that even if I weighed the same as I did in high school, I was going to look different now that I had hips and other womanly things. My dad was silent. Stab. That was my first boundary to set up with my mother, which I erected not long after this incident. I was very clear that I did not want to have one iota of a conversation with her about my weight, appearance, or looks. To this day we do not talk about it, because even when she says, "You look so pretty," I hear all the other things in her head: "but you still are fat"; "but you could be in a cuter outfit"; "but you could have lipstick on and look even cuter."

I had gone to my first Celebrate Recovery meeting two days before I was arrested and charged with DUI. Celebrate Recovery is a gathering of people who have hurts, habits, and hang-ups. The facilitators ask you on the first night why you are there. My answer: "I don't know why I'm here. Maybe anger." And two days later I was in jail. I can't even make this up. I guess my answer should have been, "I may have an alcohol problem." But was that my problem? Or was alcohol my go-to, something I used to numb the pain of my past that I wasn't dealing with? I began to process those things together—anger and alcohol. I was not naive about the effects of alcohol and about what kind of destruction the misuse of alcohol can cause in a person's life. I have been around alcoholics. For example, my grandparents were not available to attend my graduation from my Physician Assistant program because it "did not fit into their schedule." They were talking about their drinking schedule. I did not realize that their drinking had gotten to that point. Alcohol has wreaked havoc in different ways in my family. I believe that if there is an addictive (whether alcohol, drugs, sex, or tanning) gene, I probably have it for alcohol. So it's something that I have to be aware of and careful with.

When my husband and I started in our first small group with five young couples, we shared our life map. This is where you basically share the highs and lows of each stage of your life and weave them into the story of your whole life. I summed up our first year of marriage in one word: grueling. He summed it up with his own *g* word: good. Therein is the divide. And when you don't know how to bridge the divide, you cope. So that's what happened. I lived my first year of marriage feeling invalidated and controlled. I did not like it *one bit*, so I coped. With alcohol. I'd have a glass of wine because I'd had a hard day and my patients took so much of my energy. *Tonight, I'll have a glass of wine because it was a good day. Tonight, I'll have a glass of wine because my husband and I got in a fight.* And so on. We're never more creative than when we're making excuses for ourselves, right? So, on the fateful night when I was arrested, I had been at one of the best sushi restaurants in Dallas in a closed-off room listening to a lecture about toenail fungus. Not really—it was more likely about psoriasis. I was enjoying a wonderful meal with colleagues. The nice waiter was coming by and making sure my wineglass was topped off. It wasn't like I made the decision, thinking, *Okay, I'll have a second glass of wine.* Ugh, it had been too easy to drink. I hadn't even realized how much I had. I watched the video of my field sobriety test, and it looked good. I'll never forget what it felt like after I had blown into that thingamajig and the officer ripped me around, slammed my wrists together, and whacked the handcuffs on. "You have the right to remain silent. Anything you say can and will be used against you in a court of law." *Is this really happening?* I never in my wildest thoughts imagined this.

It felt like a heavy price to pay. For the next five years I had to answer yes on at least one question for my license renewal. As a medical provider there are some "biggie" questions that get asked every year including ongoing legal issues and current health and mental status. Medical boards, in this case the Texas Medical Board, did a thorough investigation of me and my case. Every two weeks I would get information in the mail about my case. The report would indicate if I needed to do anything further. I began to hate checking the mail. Sometimes I would get my husband to open those particular envelopes. I just couldn't face the bad news over and over again. It was just there, forcing me to face it. I had to hire a lawyer who would represent me in the event of a deposition. At the same time, I had a patient who filed a complaint against me because she had an allergic reaction to a topical medicine I had given her. It contained benzoyl peroxide for acne, which you can actually purchase over the counter, but that did not matter to her. I had to get letters written on my behalf by other physicians saying that I was not medically out of line, in their opinion, in my treatment plan.

This song by Nichole Nordeman was instrumental in moving me to see that the Lord's severe mercy would change me forever. He was taking me to a new place and I was not going to be able to stay where I had been anymore.

> The gate is wide, the road is paved in moderation
> The crowd is kind and quick to pull you in
> Welcome to the middle ground
> You're safe and sound and
> Until now it's where I've been

'Cause it's been fear
That ties me down to everything
But it's been love, Your love
That cuts the strings
So long status quo, I think I just let go
You make me wanna be brave
The way it always was is no longer good enough
You make me wanna be brave
Brave, brave
I am small and I speak when I'm spoken to
But I am willing to risk it all
I say Your name, just Your name
And I'm ready to jump
Even ready to fall
Why did I
Take this vow of compromise?
Why did I
Try to keep it all inside?
So long status quo, I think I just let go
You make me want to be brave
The way it always was is no longer good enough
You make me wanna be brave
Brave, brave
I've never known a fire that didn't begin with a flame
And every storm will start with just a drop of rain
But if You believe in me that changes everything
So long, I'm gone[2]

It brought tears to my eyes to learn that Nichole wrote this song after the birth of her first child, when she was not feeling particularly brave. Her firstborn was a Charlie, just like mine. In that moment of realization that it was in the midst of her suffering that she had written these words, there was hope—hope that God would use the pain of the abuse and what had been lost because of it. I also had hope that He would use my suffering in not denying the abuse any longer.

CHAPTER 2

Head Over Heels

We did fall in love. I know that happened. Mack and I met in school to become Physician Assistants at University of Texas-Southwestern in Dallas. He had shoulder-length blond hair and played soccer. I thought he was everything. He was smart, was funny, and had a smile that spread across his entire face when he was excited. Mack was the social chair of our class. I loved the gregarious, extroverted side of him that was always up for fun.

His first impression of me was that I was quiet. Great. I was on crutches the first six weeks of school after a second ACL repair surgery, so I wasn't on top of my game. We studied together all through our first year, and then we started our clinical rotations, which meant we were in two different places for four to eight weeks at a time. At some point, I think I said, "We should just say that we're dating since that's what we are doing." I wanted to talk about it because oftentimes in class or when we were around classmates he would act like he didn't know me.

He just looked at me and replied, "Nah, I think we're good." Okay.

When I started my internal medicine rotation, I and my team were on call every third night in the ER with another team. The resident on the other team was super-smart and cute. He asked me out. I very confidently (probably overconfidently) said, "Sure, I'm not dating anyone." Mack flipped out. Tearful voice mails ensued from Mack. He also made mix CDs for me. I laughed. I was like, "No, dude. I find your timing very convenient. I'm out. I'm going to see where this goes." So I dated this very important third-year resident, who is now a cardiologist, for six months.

I tried to break up with him three times once I realized that it was Mack who had my heart. The resident was so stinking smart. By the end of our discussions, he would walk away and leave me wondering what had just happened, because somehow we were not broken up. While he and I were on a walk at my parents' house over Christmas, I finally had to say, "I don't love you. I have no feelings for you. There is nowhere to go with this if I don't have that." He got it.

Journal entry, May 2, 2005

My heart hurts, Lord. And I sit here with tears in my eyes. How does our one-year anniversary turn into one of our worst nights? I told him I felt like he wasn't looking forward to dinner, that it felt like a have-to. He wanted to come and lie in bed, talk, or watch TV. That's what he was looking forward to. We went to the Grape, where we had eaten after we got engaged. Dinner was fine. We ate our wedding cake—not too bad. He had put an uncovered plate of frosting in the fridge. I made a comment, asking why it was there, and somehow I ended up a weeping mess on the kitchen floor. And I'm still weeping this morning as I sit here. Lord, I just feel tired. How can it be so different? How can it be that one year you look the most beautiful you've ever looked, exiting through a shower of sparklers at midnight, and then one year later you are crying yourself to sleep next to the same man? I have thoughts of *I can't do this.* We need help, Lord. Help. Mom prayed that Mack and I would laugh this weekend. I don't remember laughing. My heart feels squeezed this morning. It also feels bruised. I need your help, Lord, to face the day, because I don't have it in me. Sometimes I just feel like I want to stop breathing. Stop breathing. Help me to be brave.

What do you do when you are looking at your spouse thinking, *Do I love you?* Or maybe you're thinking something even scarier: *I feel like I hate you.*

As I walked out the doors of Dallas County Jail, I just remember being very thankful to be free. I was thinking that it will be very good to see Mack, and then in the same breath I realized that, based on our last twelve months of marriage, this would not be a heartwarming reunion. I did not really have the tools to temper my expectations. When I sat in the car, I felt like crying in relief. I saw his face. He was mad—mad that I had let this happen.

We have been on this marriage journey together for eleven years now, and let me tell you, it's better than this, but it is not jump-up-and-down-it's-miraculously-better-than-this. When the couple who does your premarital counseling nine years in says, "Guys, some marriages are just hard," you realize you are not going to be the poster couple for the Family Life Conference. For starters, Mack and I are two firstborns who married one another. This does not make marriage impossible, but it does make it painful. We are still the "problem children" in our small group at church. Let's just say there have been some interventions for our marriage, like, "We are coming to your house and are going to hash this out. Now. At ten o'clock at night." (I am very thankful for this.) Mack and I received couple's counseling, but we stopped attending when our second child was on the way. We have gone to several marriage conferences, and most recently we were a part of Reengage. This is a group at our church that meets weekly for sixteen weeks to help strengthen struggling marriages. Our group lovingly renamed Reengage. It is now the "My Marriage Stinks" weekly meeting. Both Mack and I found it important to be reminded about why we were in this battle fighting for our marriage. God designed it to be a relationship full of unconditional love, sacrifice, transformation—one that mirrors our relationship with him. God did not design marriage to be about our own happiness. So we think that if we're not happy, we're doing something wrong. At Reengage, we talked a lot about drawing a circle around oneself. We learned that we can't change the other person but that we can own and begin work on our own stuff. Doing this was critical for our marriage.

I do not feel like I have a daily struggle with pride. Does that mean I'm prideful? I have many other struggles, but pride has not been a biggie for me. But maybe I do struggle with pride when it comes to being with my husband. I have this entitled attitude with him: "You are my husband, and your job is to love me well, to choose me every day, and to make me feel beautiful. It's in your job description, but you are not doing it." I would frequently remind Mack of this, because I thought he needed to know. Like many men, he is not a big communicator of his feelings, the hard feelings, the ones that disappoint people. He writes well, so I would get my desire for words of affirmation when he gave me cards filled with encouraging words on my birthday, Valentine's Day, and Mother's Day (props to him). I did not receive these cards daily, but I received them enough that I felt loved. Sort of. What I realized in Reengage is that Mack's words are never going to be enough. I had this image of a deep well. Every time he did something kind—say, he took the trash out or brought me flowers—it was like one tiny drop in the well. It was huge for me to recognize the well and to say, "He doesn't owe me that." I think the well did go away immediately when I realized it was there. It was just wiped away. But let me get back to my initial point. The world reinforces this attitude of entitlement every single day: "You deserve this and that, and if he doesn't give it to you, well, then just head on out, sister! Ain't no reason to stay." Except there are a million reasons to stay. And I have five staring back at me.

The other big thing I learned at Reengage was to believe the best about my spouse. But my husband is a perfectionist and has high expectations of himself and others. It became easy for me to feel like I didn't measure up to those expectations. As much as I might wish it, I know he's not over there thinking, *I have the best wife in the world. Man, I'm lucky.* To be honest, I don't think that way about him either. A sweet, precious, dear friend of mine and I were talking. I was considering being a surrogate for her and her husband. She said the most loving thing I'd ever heard. She said, "I knew before I got married that having kids might be difficult for me, so I knew that adoption was perhaps in the future. But after we got married, I just longed to have more of him around." Oh my stars. For real. Never once had that thought crossed my mind about Mack. This was literally a foreign statement to me. And I have five children.

What I did learn at Reengage was that I could ask a question. "Hey, can you help me understand why you just said that with that tone? It sounds like you're angry. Are you?" "Can you tell me why you just closed your eyes when I was trying to tell you something?" When Mack closes his eyes, it is a *huge trigger* for me. I feel dismissed. I feel like he's closing his eyes as if willing me to stop talking and just go away. And you know what, I just want to punch him in the face. So it's fair to say I'm still learning how to believe the best about my husband.

When Mack and I were in premarital counseling, we learned about the acronym WENI. Yes, said out loud, it's "weanie." I mean, that's how it is taught: "Don't be a weanie!" The acronym is relevant to conflict and communication, and accounts for what we do in relationships. Some withdraw, some escalate, some negatively interpret, and some invalidate.[1] It troubled me to realize that Mack and I exhibited all of those behaviors. I escalate and negatively interpret, and he withdraws and invalidates. What a match made in heaven. This may explain why some marriages are "just difficult." Maybe you're already feeling better about yours. I hope so.

I got a lot of wise counsel about Mack. Most people begged me to move slowly with him. "Is he *best* for you?" was the question that kept coming up. "Are you best for each other? Does he bring out the best in you?" Don't be afraid to listen to the counsel of others around you. And even if you don't do exactly what people want you to do, consider their advice. They don't have anything to lose, but you do. You could lose everything. Mack and I took a six-week break from each other—no phone calls and no talking, just praying, asking the Lord if we were the best for each other. During that time, I prayed about three very specific things that I needed from him, three things that he did not know about:

1. To choose me and to tell others that he was choosing me
2. To be willing to spiritually lead
3. To be willing to move to Africa

We still laugh about the third one. It wasn't the thought of moving to Africa that we found funny. I still dream about doing that. I had done quite a bit of traveling to other countries. I went to El Salvador when I was twelve. Since that time, I did a one-month clinical rotation in Honduras, worked on a team that built a church in Pedro Vincente Maldonado, Ecuador, and spent a month in Antigua, Guatemala, drilling down on my Spanish, so moving to Africa was a real possibility. Mack did not address the third one specifically, but he was clear about, and knew my heart when it came to, the least of these. We decided to marry.

Our engagement story went something like this:

I knew that something was fishy when Mack said he had returned from hunting early and wanted to know if I would like to go to dinner. I asked, "Did you go hunting with Zack?"

"Uh, no. Not with. I mean, yeah, it was with Zack."

My sweet friend and roommate had been very concerned about how I looked that night, so she dressed me from her own closet. When Mack came to the door, he was very nervous. Talking fast, he said, "Let's go take a walk." We got as far as the driveway of my roommate and I's duplex when he said, "I've got good news and bad news. The bad news is that your flight for tomorrow morning is canceled. The good news is that we'll both be on it." After talking about New York City, he said, "I have one more question, Bethany Jane Lesch. Will you marry me?" The ring. Where was the ring? He found it. I couldn't see it, so he opened the Explorer's door so as to use the interior lights. We drank champagne from plastic glasses and then went to the Grape. He said he'd been planning for months to have a town car pick me up at the airport and then drive to Rockefeller Plaza, where he would be waiting and where Jackie (my sister) would be there taking photos. But a huge storm blew through NYC. After four canceled flights and a scheduling nightmare, we were booked on the same flight. So, he popped the question in the driveway of the duplex I was living in. Not exactly the engagement story you dream about it, but it has made for a great story through the years! He had certainly planned and given it every ounce of energy he had. It's like marriage. Sometimes marriage is not exactly what you dream about or picture for your life. You just have to fight for it, every day. And with children you have to fight for your marriage, and for each other, even more.

I would have been a very good single missionary. My dad must have thought so too, because he announced to a roomful of family and friends at our rehearsal dinner that he had been praying for many years that I would be just that, a single missionary. He said that my personality fit well with this role, as I am independent, perseverant, and adventurous. I was totally shocked, as was everyone else in the room. After the initial awkwardness had passed, the point was made that sometimes we don't know what's best for our children and that the Lord has a different plan. For me, I've never had a harder job than that of wife and mother. All of my junk has come to light, including the anger—O the anger. Because I was sexually abused, I often ended up in a betrayal cycle, even over little things. An offense, however great or small, would be committed, and I would feel betrayed—and then I would lash out in anger. I have been blinded by my anger. Let me say, I've never done anything harder than dig into the pain. But I tell you that there is freedom on the other side.

One of our funniest stories that Mack and I like to tell happened on a trip we'd taken long before we started dating. Mack's brother lived in Liechtenstein, a very small country bordered by Austria and Switzerland. It was supposed to be a big group going on that trip, but it ended up just being Mack and I traveling to Italy, Austria, Switzerland, and Prague on a much needed break from physician assistant school. I was dying to ride the scooters in Rome, but Mack was less than thrilled about this. He kept putting me off, until the last day we were there. We decided to do it. Things were working against us from the beginning. For one thing, it got dark in Rome at four in the afternoon. Mack thought it would be better to stay on the "smaller" streets as we learned how to ride. We showed up at a rental place run by a guy who spoke no English. He was trying to show us with motions how we were going to drive the scooter. I was to get on the back of the scooter, and then Mack would take off.

Well, we were on a cobblestone street winding through a very quaint part of Rome and were immediately met with essentially a T intersection. Mack did not make the decision about which way to turn fast enough, so we literally drove straight into a parked van at the end of the street. The owner of the van watched the whole thing go down. We sheepishly hoisted the scooter upright and waved as we drove away. Mack was so nervous that people casually walking the streets to shop or dine were turning around and staring at us as he intermittently gave the scooter some gas. Vroom, vroom, vroom. No major roads for this guy. He wanted to stay on the winding cobblestone roads with throngs of people, cafes, and shops. And, by the way, there was not another scooter in sight. We were limping along

19

and picking up a little speed when Mack decided to turn down a street that had a shop on the corner with a lovely display of vintage suitcases. Not anymore. We clipped the side of the table. I turned around and saw suitcases hurtling through the street behind us. Then I heard an angry man yelling, and I said to Mack, "Go, just go! Go!" So what did he do? He stopped the scooter in the middle of the street and turned it off. Mack and I were trying to tell the angry man that we were very sorry. He realized after about ten seconds that we were only speaking English.

The man made a dismissive sound, "Pbbbbt!" Then he waved us off as if saying, "I'm done with you! I'm done with Americans." After that, Mack and I couldn't get the scooter restarted. Our fabulous instruction had failed us. It would not start. We found a place on the sidewalk. Mack set off to find an ATM to get some cash to pay for our lovely scooter adventure. He was gone for thirty minutes. I was left feeling more and more anxious as the minutes passed. He did find an ATM. How do you think we looked *walking* up to the man's rental store as we pushed the scooter? The owner tried to make us pay for a whole front plate for the scooter, which, we realized after doing the conversion, was going to be $300. We paid him a little extra than what the rental time cost and said we wouldn't be back. He agreed. All of that is to say, Mack and I still love adventure and still travel together, which can make things very difficult when you have young children. So sometimes we have to get creative. We'll get a babysitter and try a new sushi place for date night. Or we'll stay in and watch a movie about other people having adventures. Ha, that sounds so sad. Some nights that is all we have. But listen, marriage is very hard. You gotta fight for it.

I have a dear friend who is about to make her fifth move in the ten short years she has been married. She and her husband now have three children. Their sixteen-month-old son has special needs, Down syndrome to be more specific. He is beautiful and has had many medical complications, including infantile spams, acute pancreatitis (requiring an ICU stay), and recently focal seizures. My friend's husband is a visionary. She keeps saying, "Yes, and ..." She goes with him—her heart, her mind, and her physical body all go with him and let him continue to dream. She does it beautifully. She reaches out to people in the town to which she moves, sometimes before she even gets there. She finds friends, just a couple for her and for her girls. She says, "I know right away who is going to reciprocate and who likely will not." She is undaunted by the unknowns. She is an amazing hostess. I continue to learn the art of hospitality from her. She began to see a counselor to work through her own grief with her son, which was a huge blessing, because just recently she and her husband faced the hardest trial of their marriage. She is choosing to trust the Lord, but she has wondered, *Why right now, Lord? I can't do this myself. I can't face the hardest place with a child and now with my husband at the same time.* She is digging deep and asking for the Lord's help. She said, "You know what I wish? As you're standing before the pastor on your wedding day, in your beautiful gown and with your husband in his tuxedo, I wish the pastor wouldn't say, 'Oh, isn't it so wonderful that you're getting married today and you are so happy.' I wish he would say, 'You guys are standing here in your armor. Are you ready? Are you ready for the fight, because you are both going to battle together?'" We don't always think about marriage that way, and we certainly don't think about it on those terms on our wedding day. But marriage is a battle. We are in the battle *with* each other, not against each other. We face the battle together.

Journal entry, May 29, 2014

Life is painful. I am waking up at night at 4:00 a.m., sometimes earlier. It is hard to breathe. I feel heaviness, discomfort in my own skin. Charley got left at school today for the third time. I feel like I've become that mom. Ugh. She was fine. My sweet friend went all the way back for her. I left a message to say thanks. Was that enough? Mack and I are still in a fight. It feels like it's been a week. I feel sad. Sad. I cleared away three piles of paper. No, thank you. I thought it would be fun to go to Yogurtland. He said, "Sure." We stayed for, like, seven minutes, and he did nothing to make it fun. He's the fun one. And my dreams. My dreams. No respect. He says he invited me to come sit with him on the couch, but I really was never given the choice. I said no, but I didn't reject him. I rejected the way he asked me. Pulling, commanding. Then he got hurt over the nonrejection. I can't handle living under this oppressive, critical spirit. I will not forget who I am, or the dream I feel you've laid on my heart, Lord. I think he just keeps thinking that it will all go away, that he won't have to deal with it. So I have little insight into hard things, and little idea of how to learn about myself during hard times. He just counts himself as doing some great thing because he's been thinking about me, what I would do, and what I want. It feels like he is really just thinking about himself.

On my thirty-eighth birthday, which I celebrated in 2014, I was doing the very glamorous work of picking up my daughter's immunization record for kindergarten enrollment. My two oldest daughters, seven and five, were in the car with me. I was stopped at a light counting up all of my youngest daughter's immunizations (because she asked me how many she had received). We had been sitting there for a very long time. It is legal to make a right turn on red in Texas. I guess I thought the car in front of me had gone. I eked up a little bit and bumped the car. Perfect. It was raining. A man got out of the passenger seat to look at the back of the car. I rolled down my passenger-side window because I thought he was going to come around and say something. Then the light turned green and a bus was blasting its horn because the car was not budging. I jumped out of my car and asked the car's driver to pull around into the nearby gas station if she wanted to have a discussion with me. I walked over to her car and saw that she was fired up. We talked for a few minutes. I remember that she said, "I just wanted you to acknowledge what happened."

That message stayed with me. All I could think was, *Of course*. Isn't that what we all want—to be seen, heard, and maybe even understood? And it is hard to have those conversations, isn't it? It is hard to have the painful conversations that we would rather avoid in the hopes that they will just disappear. Healing can come from those hard conversations. Healing can come when we understand that the person who seems different from us really is not that different after all.

CHAPTER 3

Embracing Our Differences

I'm a Physician Assistant in dermatology. I was talking to my oldest daughter about the first time that I did a punch biopsy on a woman with dark skin. I take a 4 mm circular area of the skin down to the fat, and then I close up the wound with one or two sutures. I have done this procedure thousands of times since, but the first time has stayed with me. It stayed with me because I lifted the piece of skin out of the patient's arm and was like, *Oh my word, it looks exactly like mine.* Skin consists of epidermis and dermis. I just assumed that the dermis of this dark-skinned person would have melanin (pigment-producing cells) in it as well. No, the dermis was stark white. All of a sudden, in that moment, I thought, *What in the world? Our forefathers decided that a dark-skinned man gets 3/5 of a vote. Someone decided that a woman has to be a slave because of epidermis 1 millimeter thick that has more melanin in it than mine* (.05 mm thickness on the eyelids and 1.5 mm on the palms and soles, so 1 mm is an average. It's the thickness of your fingernail.) I told my daughter this story because I thought it made for an interesting teaching point. This was before I came to her class and read *Beatrice's Goat* written by Page McBrier and beautifully illustrated by Lori Lohstoeter. *Beatrice's Goat* is a beautiful story about a little girl in Uganda whose family receives a goat, which allows the girl to go to school for the first time. My daughter hadn't seemed all that interested in my discussion, but then she came home from school and said, "Mom, I told Damon* that you said our skin is exactly the same, that he has white skin too—it's just underneath." O.M.Goodness. I was silenced and then felt panic begin to creep in. And I was like, *Here we go. Let the e-mails abound. I'm going down.*

To make a long story short, I e-mailed Damon's* mom. She and I met and had coffee. Hallelujah! She did not bring that story up, but I sat mesmerized by hers. She used to live in the Congo. Her entire family is still there. Her husband came to the United States, and she waited a year to find out if she could come and join him. She now has lived in the states for three years with her three children. Her husband works several states away, so she functions as a single mom for three out of four weeks a month. She works tirelessly and sends a significant amount of money back to her family. She said, "It's good here because my husband and I are a team. Not like an African husband." I asked her what that meant, and she said, "Oh, an African husband in the middle of the night would wake me up and say, 'Go get some water for me.'" She said that her sister's husband "put her out" for something minor, which means that he put her out of the house and she could not return until he allowed her to. Both families, nine *months* later, went through a ritual of killing a goat and then all ate it together. The sister asked for forgiveness, and the sister's husband's family received it (they had the option to refuse). Then she was allowed back in her home. Women seem to not be valued for the very important role they fill as wife and mother. She said that she had been praying for a friend and that I was an answer to her prayer. She was an answer to mine.

In our modern, enlightened society, why is racism still happening? I read the majority of the Department of Justice report on Ferguson, Missouri. I realize that this is a highly political hot-button issue, but you know what, it's happening. It's still happening, and not just in Missouri. It's all around us. People are being profiled, charged, and convicted because they are African American.

> African Americans are 2.07 times more likely to be stopped in a vehicular stop but are 26% less likely to have contraband on them during a search. African Americans account for 95% of all Manner of Walking charges; 94% of all Failure to Comply charges; 92% of all Resisting Arrest charges; 92% of all Peace Disturbance charges and 89% of all Failure to Obey charges. African Americans are 68% less likely than others to have their case dismissed by the municipal judge and in 2013 African Americans

accounted for 92% of cases in which an arrest warrant was issued.

And later on the report concludes, "The racially disparate impact of Ferguson's practices is driven, at least in part, by intentional discrimination in violation of the Equal Protection Clause of the Fourteenth Amendment. Racial bias and stereotyping is evident from the facts, taken together."[1] And there was no avenue to bring a complaint against an officer. This sounds like a developing country, not our blessed America.

There typically seems to be much discussion about how racism is taught. I read a blog post by Maria Dixon Hall, a professor at the University of Oklahoma, who spoke out after the SAE fraternity brothers were taped singing racial slurs on the way to a function. She says that racism is a "congenital heart condition," but she is very clear in stating that a child doesn't have to have a parent who shouts racial slurs in order to become a racist. "Children learn from what their parents don't say," Hall explains. "Young white adults suffer myocardial infarctions of bigotry when their churches either ignore race by erasing it or frame people of color as 'objects of mission' rather than collaborators in the Great Commission." She then challenges the current wisdom by writing that another, appropriate consequence would have been to have the young men sing the song live in front of Walter, the man who has cooked meals at the SAE house for the last fifteen years. She would have had Walter ask, "Is this really what you think of me?" Her argument is that the fraternity brothers would have answered no. She says, "The human conscious is a most powerful ally in the battle for social justice." She goes on to discuss Martin Luther King's enduring stance stipulating that while the law allows black people and white people to sit together at the same table, "only the Gospel of Jesus Christ could heal the heart condition known as racism." Without the Holy Spirit guiding our words, thoughts, and actions, our efforts to live in true fellowship would be shallow and superficial, Hall alleges. She goes on to say, "Our knee-jerk reactions to the subject of race reveal our great discomfort with real conversation regarding how this sad legacy continues to affect us all."[2] And it is sad. It's sad that overt racism continues. I would argue that my generation has *no* excuse for being racist. It's sad to me that I'm convicted when I read that what parents don't say also has an effect. I want my children to believe that blacks and whites are equal in value; we are people on a mission who want what is best for our families. I want my children to believe that blacks and whites are equals, just like women are equal to men. We are all co-laborers on a mission. We are *all* told to go out and to be a light. The world needs all of us.

It's not the first time that women have reached out to one another across racial lines. At the turn of the twentieth century, white and black women came together for what cause? Women came together to fight against slavery. After reading the new Jim Crow law, I don't find it too difficult to make the leap that in this day and age, the equivalent would be women coming together to fight against racism. These women were not just holding up signs for their cause; they were walking arm in arm through violent opposition and the burning buildings where they once held meetings. Are we brave enough? Are we brave enough to stand with our sisters? These women were progressive and were undeterred by their opposition. There were many who disagreed with abolishing slavery. But these women stood together. Are we willing to stand with and for each other? These women were called the Abolitionist Sisterhood. I'm dreaming about what that would look like today.

Michelle Alexander's *The New Jim Crow* struck a chord with me in a painful, sobering way. To be honest, before I entered into the public health world in 2010, I would have said that racism in our country was virtually nonexistent. I mean, my grandfather refused to buy Japanese cars and he used slang words when speaking about minorities, but in my book he was one of the worst offenders. He just seemed antiquated to me. But my generation? They have no excuse. We don't use racial slurs. One of my favorite counselors at camp was black. I liked the black the kids in my high school (the select few who were mostly athletes). I worked as a counselor for Kids Across America (an urban ministry at Kanakuk Kamps) one summer while I was in college. I know, it sounds so anemic. What I realized from my public health education is that I do not have the first clue as to the unique and pervasive inequalities that exist for any and all minorities in this country. One of the hardest parts of Alexander's book is when she discusses the devastating effects that the mass incarceration of young black men has had on their families and communities. During slavery and, later, the civil rights movement, black communities came together and were stronger in their fight against the atrocities that befell them. Now, imprisonment brings shame to the families that it affects, so those families remain silent. Their suffering is in isolation, because they do not feel the freedom to come to their families or church communities to share. It is one more devastating obstacle for families who have already lost their daddy, brother, uncle, or son.

Alexander writes the following:

> The idea that we may never reach a state of perfect racial equality—a perfect racial equilibrium—is not cause for alarm. What is concerning is the real possibility that we, as a society, will choose not to care. ... Seeing race is not the problem. Refusing to care for the people we see is the problem. ... We should hope not for a colorblind society but instead for a world in which we can see each other fully, learn from each other, and do what we can to respond to each other in love. That was King's dream—a society that is capable of seeing each of us, as we are, with love. That is a goal worth fighting for. ... If we had actually learned to show love, care, compassion, and concern across racial lines during the Civil Rights Movement—rather than go colorblind—mass incarceration would not exist today. ... We have allowed ourselves to be willfully blind to the emergence of a new caste system—a system of social ex-communication that has denied millions of African Americans basic human dignity. The significance of this cannot be overstated, for the failure to acknowledge the humanity and dignity of all persons has lurked at the root of every racial caste system.[3]

I recently watched a bold documentary, *Compelling Love*, which has a different subject—homosexuality—but a similar issue. Homosexuals are also a marginalized group. In the documentary, many people who live a homosexual lifestyle explain that it is very easy to tell when they are being "tolerated." They make the point they do not want to be merely tolerated. They are human beings, and they want to be treated as such. And what do we all inherently want? To be respected and loved. How do we respect those who are different from us? How do we love each other? How do we listen to each other? How do we find common ground to be kind to one another? It's what we are called to do. John 1:9–15 reads, "The true light that gives light to everyone was coming into the world. He was in the world, and though the world was made through him, the world did not recognize him. He came to that which was his own, but his own did not receive him. Yet to all who did receive him, to those who believed in his name, he gave the right to become children of God-children born not of natural descent, nor of human decision or a husband's will, but born of God." If we believe in his name, then we are *all* his children. Later in that same chapter, Jesus says, "You believe because I told you I saw you under the fig tree. You will see greater things than that." Did you get that? Jesus, the Son of God, is saying that *you* will see greater things than he has done! Listen. He's calling you.

Jesus loved women and treated them as if they were important and had important things to contribute. That's the God I serve. That's why I would call myself a Jesus feminist. "We are creating a world where every woman can be who she is, without apology, in freedom. For the sake of the gospel, women must speak—and teach and minister and prophesy, too. For the sake of the gospel, a woman must be free to walk in her God-breathed self in whatever vocation and season and place of life."[4] Hallelujah!

I was telling my mom about the book *Jesus Feminist*, and she asked me what the term meant. "I don't know exactly yet, but I'm reading the book and I love it. Jesus loved women. For his time, he was a radical in how he treated women specifically." Yes, rise up. Women, rise up. I didn't grow up in the sixties. I was born in 1977, so I don't carry the baggage of the negative connotations surrounding the word *feminist*. I did look up some information and found that, ironically, the alleged bra burnings seem not to have actually happened. Who knew? Women took off their bras and other iconic female items, including girdles and corsets, and dumped them into a "Freedom" trash can at the Miss America pageant in 1968, but no burning occurred. Lindsy Van Gelder wrote a piece comparing the trash can incident to the burning of draft cards at antiwar marches—and that is how the myth was born. So it appears that women burning their bras wasn't actually a thing. Good to know.

My church came out with print material that read, "What it means to be God's man" and "What it means to be God's woman." It sounded great; I couldn't wait to walk through this with my kids. I love my church, have the utmost respect for the pastor, and trust the leadership of the elders, so I couldn't figure out at first what about these materials was not sitting well with me. And just as a point of reference, this is still my church home. I haven't left it and I'm not going to. I am just being honest about the stirrings in my heart for God's women.

I read how to be God's man:

1. Step up.
2. Speak out.
3. Stand strong.
4. Stay humble.
5. Serve the King.

Yes, I loved it all. But then I was like, *Why is there another list? This is the list. These things are what God wants. This is what I want for myself. This is what I want my* sons *and* daughters *to do. Yes, Lord, give us the courage to do this.* What do you think I read on the other list indicating how to be God's woman?

1. Seek God first.
2. Speak faithfully.
3. Show true beauty.
4. Stay humble.
5. Serve the Lord.

And now I was fuming! This was *clearly* a list authored by a man. These are all great things, but why the distinction? Shouldn't we all speak out and stand strong? I think so. In my mind, nothing is more beautiful than standing strong. And as men and women, we should speak out faithfully. I'm talking about speaking out for the Lord, not just speaking out to speak out. I can still fear the Lord (Proverbs 31:30) and be steadfast, immovable, always abounding in the work of the Lord, knowing that my toil is not in vain in the Lord (1 Corinthians 15:58). Proverbs 31:8–9 reads, "Open your mouth for the mute, for the rights of all the unfortunate. Open your mouth, judge righteously and defend the rights of the afflicted and needy."

Isn't that my job too? And am I not called as well to "rescue those being led away to death; [to] hold back those staggering toward slaughter"? The Scripture goes on to state, "If you say, But we knew nothing about this, does not he who weighs the heart perceive it? Does not he who guards your life know it? Will he not repay everyone according to what they have done" (Proverbs 24:11–12)? I will seek God first as I step up. My pastor had written, "Step up" (Lead. Initiate. Be a man of action. Assume it is your job and your moment. Hate apathy. Reject passivity). I will be honest, to the shock and horror of some, and say that there is something about this that feels paternalistic. Women are to lead, initiate, be people of action, assume it their job and their moment, hate apathy, and reject passivity, too. We lead our families every day as we initiate what is best for our children. Many women lead in professional settings. We should also be leading on the global stage. If the church is going to make an impact on its people, then it needs to release and empower all of its people, including the oh-so-important population of women. For all of the progress the church has made, I will admit that I am tired of feeling held back. I am tired of the assertion that speaking out and standing strong are not things that I should be doing. I do not think it is loving to send this message. If Elisabeth Elliot can go back to the Waorani Indians who killed her husband and share the gospel, resulting in a third of the tribe (around two thousand men and women) receiving the Lord as their Savior, then how much more are all women called? Elliot said, "My reason for being a missionary was one of the few things I had never doubted. I knew one thing—I must obey God, and I believed this was the thing He meant me to do, just as He meant others to be fishermen … draftsmen, housewives. The role seemed incidental. The goal was all-important." Two of my other favorite quotes from Elisabeth Elliot are, "There is nothing worth living for, unless it is worth dying for" and "The secret is Christ in me, not me in a different set of circumstances."[5] She was a radical in 1952, and she probably is still considered radical today. I'm not sure I know a mother who (widowed) would take her only daughter, a precious three-year-old, with her into the jungle to spread the gospel of Jesus. Elliot was a radical for forgiveness. I believe we need more people like her today.

I know one woman who is thankful that she stepped up. Her name is Goretti, and she lives in northern Burundi. A mother of six, she was regularly beaten by her husband and not allowed to go to the market by herself. On her own accord and without her husband's approval, she became a part of the CARE program with about twenty other women in her village. These women work together, rotating whose field they farm. Goretti was able to buy fertilizer, which helped her produce a wonderful potato crop. She now has a business making banana beer, and she owns two goats. She explained that there is an expression regarding women in relation to men: "A hen cannot speak in front of a rooster." Now she says that she and other women speak up and are a part of the community. Bernard, her husband, said that he is much happier with a partner than a servant. Goretti said, "I used to underestimate myself, but now I tell people what I think."[6] That's right, you go, girl!

I read *Half the Sky* by Nicholas Kristof and Sheryl WuDunn before I began work on my Master of Public Health, and I think the former was a catalyst for my pursuing the latter. The title of the book comes from a Chinese proverb that says that women hold up half the sky. My sister knew about the book because she works for the International Justice Mission, which is discussed in the book, so I decided to read it—and I loved it. The sentence that blew me away that still stays with me is, "If there is to be a successful movement on behalf of women in poor countries, it will have to bridge the God Gulf. Secular bleeding hearts and religious bleeding hearts will have to forge a common cause. That's what happened two centuries ago in the abolitionist movement, when liberal deists and conservative evangelicals joined forces to overthrow slavery. And it's the only way to muster the political will to get now-invisible women onto the international agenda." All I could think was, *Yes* ... but how in the world is that possible? You know what's interesting? Christians are the ones who get blasted for being judgmental and narrow-minded, but you know what? I'm not mad at anyone for thinking differently than I do. I'm not angry with a person because he or she is not a Christian and does not believe in Jesus. I can respect the fact that others have a different set of beliefs. I'm happy to enter into a conversation with non-Christians, and it does not make me angry that we think differently.

Why the vitriol? Is it just because we think about things differently? We are human beings. It's interesting to shift one's perspective over time. I grew up in a very conservative home. (Let's just say that for Christmas, I bought a mug for my dad that reads, "Right-wing nut job.") My sister and I have a bit of a more socially liberal viewpoint these days. My dad feels very strongly against abortion, believing that life starts at conception. And I get it. I don't disagree. But guess what I learned? The other school of thought is not necessarily pro-death. Do you know what they are thinking about? They are thinking of the baby that is born to a fifteen-year-old mother who may not know who the father is and has very few resources to sustain the child. Is she going to continue on in school? Can she afford the formula so that the baby does not fail to thrive? Does she have a support system to help her when the dad doesn't want to play an active role in the baby's life? What about abuse and neglect? My question is, where are the conservative Christians when it comes to doing these things? We are working really hard to get women to keep their babies, but what are we doing to support them in that decision? Are we adopting the child when a woman decides to give a baby up? What are we *doing* to help the babies and moms to live, to merely survive, not necessarily thrive? Where are we?

So, the question still at hand is, how do we bridge the "God gulf"? If I read too much of what the media report, I get discouraged. It feels like everyone is just firing grenades. If you listen, you discover that everyone is complaining about the same thing. You know how I think we may be able bridge the God gulf? We do it by approaching one another with the *assumption* that we will learn something new. So, this involves listening to one other. Don't think that you know that person across the table. Friends of the Christian variety, don't look at that person and assume that he or she has no moral compass. Non-Christians do have a moral compass. Learn something from them. You may hear a story of pain and suffering. Friends, don't assume that the Christian across the table from you is a bigoted, narrow-minded lunatic. Ask Christians why they believe what they believe. You may hear a story of pain and suffering. You may hear a story of grace. I have learned a lot from hearing what people who are different from me think. For example, I have heard the idea of making oral contraceptives become available over the counter instead of requiring a prescription. I can hear my Christian friends now: "What has this world come to? Everyone is having sex, and it's just going to start younger and younger." Guess why some people may be in favor of making birth control pills available over the counter? Doing so will help prevent pregnancies, teenage or otherwise. Making contraceptive tablets available over the counter takes away the obstacle of the required visit to a health care provider (and being one myself, I should be recommending that people do this). Someone could make a responsible choice and stop by his or her local pharmacy instead. Do you know that it is difficult to visit a health care provider for some? It costs money and time. On top of that, some people don't even know where to go. And by the way, making oral contraceptives available without a prescription does not cause people to want to have sex. Come to the table and be ready to learn something new, something that will make you think. There are two sides to the story. I promise.

You know what? Christians have far from cornered the market on loving others well. I've met some Christians who I wish were not Christians. (I mean, go to heaven, fine, but don't act crazy and tell people that you know Jesus.) Let's be honest, we Christians are often terrible at loving others. We don't act like Jesus would have. He was winsome, grace-filled, and brave, always meeting others' needs before his own. Unfortunately, that's often not us. We act ugly, selfish, and angry, and that never goes over well. So, yeah, I have met people about whom I've thought, *Man, oh man, I wouldn't want to be a Christian if that's what being a Christian looks like.* And I may have been that type of person once (or, cough, twice). I still remember a sweet lady in the post office whom I should have helped but I didn't. How are we going to respond to the homosexual people in our lives? They are human beings with feelings, and we are called to refrain from casting the first stone. Remember what John 8 discusses: let him with no sin cast the first stone. And there was not one among the crowd who was without sin. I am not any different. You are not any different. Remember the baker who refused to bake a cake for her homosexual patron's wedding? I understand that if it is her business, she should be able to decide whom she is going to do business with, but I'm just not sure whom that helps. It just comes across as being judgmental. Go call your congressman or rally in the streets if you want a change. I'm just not sure how it is helpful to anyone to refrain from loving a friend well. Apparently, this woman and her customer had known each other for fifteen years. That's more than an acquaintance. And sometimes loving your friend is communicating hard things, things that the other person may not want to hear, but sometimes it's just loving them right where they are. That group of friends that you are communicating hard things with for each of us is very small, maybe one, two, or three people. And remember, if you are going to communicate those hard things to a friend, then you better be ready to receive similar exhortation. The hard things I'm talking about are people who are asking about your marriage, about how you are doing with your kids (really doing), about if you are using alcohol or food (or anything else for that matter) to make you feel better. So, go rally in the streets for your cause *and* love your friend well too. Friends love each other. I think Jesus would have baked the cake. I also think he would have hosted a party for his homosexual friend who was getting married, too. Oh, that's right, he actually did that. He hosted a party for the sinners, including tax collectors (Mark 2). You should love the person who is right in front of you, whom you know or don't know. Listen to his or her story; ask about his or her journey. You may learn something new.

In my journal on May 15, 2002, I glued in verses from Isaiah 61:1–4, as follows:

> Spirit of the Lord God is upon me,
> because the Lord has anointed me
> to bring good news to the poor;
> he has sent me to bind up the brokenhearted,
> to proclaim liberty to the captives,
> and the opening of the prison to those who are bound;
> to proclaim the year of the Lord's favor,
> and the day of vengeance of our God;
> to comfort all who mourn;
> to grant to those who mourn in Zion—
> to give them a beautiful headdress instead of ashes,
> the oil of gladness instead of mourning,
> the garment of praise instead of a faint spirit;
> that they may be called oaks of righteousness,
> the planting of the Lord, that he may be glorified.
> They shall build up the ancient ruins;
> they shall raise up the former devastations;

they shall repair the ruined cities,
the devastations of many generations.

Maybe let's be willing to get uncomfortable, even crossing over lines that we have been afraid to cross. Sweet Katie Davis. What I love about Katie is that she does not think that she's doing anything extraordinary. "God taught me, over and over, that it did not matter what the world said, that it did not matter that almost none of the people closest to me believed in what I was doing or believed it would succeed, that it did not matter what they said was impossible, because God did this and he was going to continue doing it." And we listen to those other people, don't we? They know us and love us, and we are looking for direction. So we listen. Davis goes on to write the following:

> I didn't realize then, but I strongly believe now that there is a common misconception that whatever happens to us is the will of God. *It's as though we think: Okay, I can do whatever I want and God will either do something or He won't and that will be His will. It will all work out. It will all happen just like it needs to.* I don't believe this anymore. I believe that God is in control, yes, but I also believe I have a choice: I can follow Him or I can turn my back on Him. I can go to the hard places or I can remain comfortable. And if I remain comfortable, God who loves us unconditionally will continue to love me anyway. I may still see His glory revealed in my life and recognize His blessings, but not like I could have. I can miss the will of God.[7]

I couldn't agree more. If I fight really hard to make things be comfortable or easy, I will miss what God has for me, I believe. And I don't want to miss it.

PART 2

The Tension We Experience while Working (as Moms)

What is the rudest question you can ask a woman, "How do you juggle it all?" "You're jacking it all up, aren't you?" their eyes say.[1]

Tina Fey

CHAPTER 4

The Demanding "Should Do" List

The "should do" list my counselor encouraged me to write looked like this:

> I should exercise daily. I should spend time with the Lord every day. I should lovingly discipline my kids. I should have dinner ready on the days I am home. I should have sex with my husband at least once a week. I should be involved with my kids and their school. I should be an excellent physician assistant (PA). I should complete my husband. I should continue my work at University of Texas-Southwestern. I should finish the online dermatology PA project [a professional project one volunteers to do] even though it will now be extended six months. I should spend more time with my kids. I should provide fun, engaging activities for my kids inside and outside the home. I should tell other people about Jesus. I should be a diligent student. I should be available as a friend and sister. I should finish my master's degree in a reasonable amount of time. I should serve regularly in my church, be in a community group, and be accountable to the women. I should help the poor. I should breast-feed my child for a year. I should not work outside the home full-time. I should drink only on special occasions. I should not be angry. I should not discipline my kids

when I am angry. I should not spend extra time outside
the home if it can be avoided. I should not be angry with
my husband when I feel invalidated and unloved. I should
not be angry when my ideas, thoughts, dreams, or visions
are dismissed by my husband. I should not have dreams
or goals at the expense of my family. I should not escalate
or negatively interpret.

One of my favorite patients is Miss C. The pillar of her family, she
grew up with a "should do" list that could have left her bitter, but she
overcame. In high school, she dreamed of becoming an airline stewardess.
She received a scholarship, but her mother refused to allow her to go for
the training because she was afraid that she would die in a plane crash. Miss
C. dreamed of going to college and had a family member who was willing
to help her go, but her mom refused because she needed her to work in
the local jean factory to support the family. She married at eighteen and
became a victim of domestic violence. She left that marriage and married
again at age twenty. She has worked as a bank clerk, proof operator, ostrich
farmer, baker, home health nurse, and funeral director. She has now been
married for thirty-six years, and for thirty of those years she has cared for
her husband, who has had two heart attacks, colon cancer, prostate cancer,
and cholesterol problems. She is raising her granddaughter, who is twelve
now, because her son is having marital problems. She traveled back and
forth from Dallas to Oklahoma to care for her mother, who refused to
move closer to her daughter, until her death last year. She went back to
school this year to become a community health worker (CHW), enrolling
in the first program of its kind in our state. Community health workers
are the wave of the future in regard to how health care is implemented
in this market, and Miss C. is on the front line. She wrote, "My life has
been hard, never really feeling that I was truly loved, but through God I
know he is my savior and I am one of his children. I could go on more,
but I'm not looking for sympathy, I just wanted to be understood."[1] And
if you met her, you would say, "I have just met a kind and gentle soul, not
an angry or bitter woman." Walk on, warrior woman.

I completely crashed when the twins turned six months old. The
words that had carried me into their births, "Now, child you are ready for

what I have for you. You are ready to become the mama I will make you to be,"² were lost in the back of my mind. You rally early on after giving birth because you know that despite that fact that it's going to be very hard and you are not going to get much sleep, it is going to get better. I think I crashed because the harsh reality was that this was my family's new normal and it felt very hard.

In August 1999, I was in the middle of Pedro Vincente Maldonado, Ecuador, when I wrote, "The wind ripped through my hair and the beautiful countryside passed by and as I held sleeping Dina [one of the young Quicha girls] with only a three-inch metal ridge to keep me from hurtling to my death. I knew this was freedom, something that I could do." I was twenty-two years old. I was on a team with one American and about twelve Britons in the middle of Ecuador serving Quicha Indians and helping them build their church (a cross-cultural experience). We slept on the ground, bathed in the river one mile away, pooped in a hole, and had intermittent electricity. We got our food at the local market and rotated cooking duty. And in that same pickup truck, on the trip back from the market, which took three hours, we sang. The whole way back, we huddled together and kept singing. We sang even louder when it started raining. We sang songs from *Grease*. We sang the English national anthem to the tune of "My Country 'Tis of Thee" ("My country 'tis of thee, sweet land of liberty, of thee I sing. Land where my fathers died, land of the pilgrims' pride, from every mountainside, let freedom ring." Let freedom ring.

Journal entry, January 26, 2014

Feeling desperate. Tears. At the lake. Cool. I hear the waves and seagulls. Maybe I could just fly away with them. Just for a day. I am thankful it's not cries, screams, or the 437th question of the day. I am weary. I didn't know it would be this hard. I didn't know I would feel this alone. I have friends with kids who are getting older. I know parents who want to hear the good stuff and don't know what to do with the heartache. I have kids who are relentless in their needs. I have a husband who can't possibly fill the void. I know, Lord, that you are here. I know that you love me. I know that you care. I know you hear me. I just feel crazy sometimes. Literally crazy. I did get to exercise yesterday; that was a blessing. It does help me to dream. I think that something bigger than my small world could be happening, that you, Lord, could be leading somehow, some way, like you did in Jennie Allen's heart. So clear. Gather and equip your generation. And the IF:Gathering is happening. Lord, you helped her do it. Wow. All I can think is that there will be years of work for Mack to get to the place where he will release me to go! I pray right now, Lord, that you would begin to move, to stir in his heart to set me free. As I sat in the car crying, I heard the songs "Everlasting God (Strength Will Rise) by Chris Tomlin and "Open Hands, Broken Hallelujah" by the Afters. I'm on my knees, Lord. I trust you as I breathe, as I take one breath at a time. Because I can't do anything else. Because I am overwhelmed by the magnitude of my responsibility. Charley—exceedingly high expectations, unrelenting questions; Kate—fragile, dramatic when it comes to bumps and bruises, not eating well, still taking her pacifier to bed; Sam—still crying when he should be talking, hitting and not sharing, wants toys everyone else has, keeps getting sick; Sarah—teething, up in the middle of the night, needs full attention, and can hold me hostage-like Charley and Crew—up in the night when the pacifier comes out. Ho-hum. Poor me. Hit gratitude journal.

Journal entry, August 26, 2008

Wow. One year ago today I was sitting in a hospital bed after having fainted in the bathroom from volume depletion (eighteen hours of labor and no epidural—that's another story), no sleep, bleeding (with a stage-three tear), and sitting on ice with this sweet, precious baby I had no idea what to do with. What a difference a year makes! I feel so thankful for her and for where we are. There are some things that feel hard. She's not a baby anymore. I've cried about that. Such sweet times those several months after. You are just consumed with this new precious life. Single-minded. Taking care of her. God, you are good. Now she's a big girl. Almost walking. Help us, Father. And thank you. Thank you for the miracle of her life.

I read *Mission of Motherhood*[3] before my first child was born. I remember that it made me feel inspired and challenged for the task of raising a child. I knew it wouldn't be easy, but I felt up for it. I was not operating under the illusion that it would always be buttercups and rainbows. I knew that there would be more difficult days. Before my first daughter was born, I remember thinking that the hardest parts of motherhood for me would be the relentless aspect of children (they are always there) and then the inability to reason to reason with them (e.g., "Sam, why are you screaming about not having pizza on your plate when you said you didn't want it?").

The Highly Sensitive Child by Elaine Aron, PhD, was a life source for me as I parented my oldest daughter. I really felt that either I was crazy or she was—I wasn't sure. Aron describes highly sensitive individuals as those who are born with a tendency to notice more in their environment and deeply reflect on everything before acting. She explains that a key part of accepting your child is admitting the things that seem strange, frustrating, and disappointing. "All of this has to be grieved. You may never send this child to summer camp, or see her as a team captain, or have the phone ringing off the hook with party invitations, or see her being immediately happy and spontaneous in new settings."[4] I cried when I read that. I loved summer camp and was concerned that my daughter may never get to go. It seemed so trite. I mean, she was three years old. Grieving nonetheless happened, but it was more about my failures, how I had failed to love my daughter well because I did not understand her. It took thirty minutes to get her ready for soccer practice ... every week. I look back and I wonder, *What were we doing? Why did we not just stop?* I think that early on, it probably would have been better for my daughter if I had pulled her from soccer, because it was just so exhausting. Part of it was that she was my husband's and my first child. Maybe every kid hates shin guards? She fought tooth and nail, *every* step. We got the ones that have the shin guard attached to the ankle cuff. Big mistake. Once I presented those to her, it ended in a screaming disaster. And her socks had to be perfectly aligned. Usually the seam needed to be just underneath her toe or else it would bother her. The laces had to be just right, not too snug but not too loose. And all of that sounds fine, but there were usually tears. I didn't understand. When does a parent lovingly push a child, and when does a parent say, "Okay, we are throwing in the towel"? Again, I will err on the sound of pushing her too hard, so I have to be careful. My family has come up with the rule that if one of us starts something, he or she is going to finish it, whether that's soccer season or gymnastics class.

Pregnancy is a lot like a marathon. It's like the greatest test your body goes through. Throughout the pregnancy, your body has been wholly focused on one glorious goal, finishing the race. You often put every ounce of energy into keeping your body healthy and strong, making wise nutrition choices along the way and staying hydrated, staying focused, and finishing strong.

I've run one marathon. I've been pregnant four times. So let's call it five. I've run five marathons.

I love being pregnant. I have a sweet friend who reminded me that I had said I loved being pregnant, because sometimes I forget it. It's actually true. I don't get morning sickness (I know: you want to stab me in both my eyes), and I just feel more energized. I think of pregnancy like a marathon. I mean, it really is, right? A pregnancy lasts ten months (forty weeks) from start to finish, even though the common knowledge is that it lasts nine months. I hope I'm not the first person to break this news to you.

As I mentioned, I've run a marathon, only one to date. It was the Marine Corps Marathon in Washington, DC, in October 2006. This marathon is as intense as it sounds. You have marines, some of the most physically fit people you'll ever see, running alongside you. It's hard not to be intimidated, right? I sometimes felt as if everyone else had trained harder than I, that everybody was more ready than I. *Can I even do this, finish the race?* Doubt ran through my mind. Oh man, it was grueling—beautiful, but grueling. You run through Georgetown, down beautiful Rock Creek Parkway, through all the monuments, and past Capitol Hill, and then you take a bit of a downturn through Potomac Park, head back up through Crystal City, run along the Potomac, and finally finish. I trained hard, I was ready, and I hit the wall at mile 14. Yes, mile 14, which meant I had 12.2 miles to go. I trained with Luke's Locker in Dallas, one of the leaders in running and fitness, through the entire blistering summer. We started our long runs at a quarter to six in the morning when the temperature outside was often ninety degrees. When we finished, it was usually over one hundred degrees. It was a record-breaking extreme-temperature kind of a summer. I have never sweat so much in my life. I mean that I was drenched, head to toe—even my shoes. I remember feeling that way about breast-feeding too, like everything in me was being poured out for this little one's life. I digress. I still remember the squish, squish, squish of my shoes as I was walking back to my car after finishing the race. It was like every last drop of me had been poured out. I had trained for five months, running four or five days a week, with my long runs on Saturdays. I had new shoes, but not too new (they had 30 miles on them), and I had trained with my GU Chomps (much preferred to the energy gel, which tied my stomach in knots). I was ready. I was fired up, but I still crashed. My sister ran a long way with me, my dad ran almost 14 miles with me, and one of my sweet training partners who was not in the race ran alongside me through the last five miles. And let's not forget the last 0.2 mile, because it was uphill to the Iwo Jima Memorial. Killer. So sometimes, even when you're ready, you crash. Sometimes you get to the end of your pregnancy and you crash. You're just so ready to meet this little life and to have your body back again. (Oh, right, that second part will take a while—for some of us, it will be longer than for others.) Please do not have the expectation that your body will return to its pre-pregnancy state in six or even twelve weeks. I think that happens to about 0.2 percent of the female population, and they are all blogging about it. No judgment here; more power to them. And many are doing it in a very healthy way. Some of us who may have only gained twenty-five pounds in pregnancy have never gotten back to where we were before we were pregnant. Let me just say that in my case it has not been for lack of trying. I eat healthy 80 percent of the time (I know, that's my problem), and I exercise regularly. Both of those things have looked different to me over time, especially since I've birthed babies. I have historically been a runner. I ran in high school and have enjoyed running for exercise throughout the years. I spent nine months training at Camp Gladiator (three days a week for an hour each) starting when the twins were five months old. And now I, my husband, and a few of our friends have been knocking out thirty minutes of hard-core exercise with Shaun T in my driveway. First Mack and I had a Focus T25 baby, and now we've graduated to Insanity Max 30—it's crazy. We do it five days a week. I felt like I was just maintaining my weight, as I haven't lost any pounds. No one is saying, "Oh, girl, you look so good!" Not one person. Sometimes we work very hard with little visible results. Huh, that sounds a lot like motherhood on a daily basis. Sometimes we face the fear (even the fears of mothering), we accomplish the goal, we finish the race, and there is victory.

I'd like to set the record straight about one of the most widely held misconceptions. As I mentioned before, pregnancy lasts ten months, not nine. It's forty weeks from start to finish. That's the way the battle often is—harder and longer than anyone will give you credit for. I see you, warrior woman.

Journal entry, June 30, 2009

What a day, and it's only 1:30 p.m. At thirty-six weeks pregnant, I woke up with seven bites. Charley was a whiny pistol from the moment she got up. I yelled at her at 8:30, saying that she was not going to act like this. (She was crying about everything. I put her in her pink tutu. Then she wanted to wear the green one. I put that on her. Then she wanted the pink one again.) Mama put her foot down. Got to Dr. N's office early. After I entertained Charley for thirty minutes, she was done about the time Dr. N was ready to see me. Charley threw the iPod across the floor. The speaker shattered. The iPod went through the door and into the hallway. For the next five minutes, I tried to get Charley some goldfish crackers and an iPod video while my OB was getting a Group B strep swab and checking to see if I was dilated. (This is what we do, right?) She also commented on my lovely varicose vein.

Awesome. I was late getting Charley to swim class. She does have fun. Victory! She pooped in the swim diaper. So I took off everything she was wearing. I dumped the poop in the toilet while trying to clean the rest off in the toilet water (multiple flushes). It got on both of us, so we both got in the shower. Afterwards, I got her wet suit and diaper back on. While I was driving to the spray park, I was running late. I got pulled over by the speed trap cops, who were on foot. I was driving fifty-three miles per hour when the speed limit was forty. The cops had stopped five others by the time I turned around. The spray park was fun—Michelle, Miriam, Kim, Ashley, and Kristin were there. I'm thankful to be home and with a child who's napping. I just have to laugh. Thank you, Lord, for a good swim class. Thank you for a child who poops. Thank you for friends. Thank you for a good appointment. Heart rate is 150. It felt like the baby has turned. I am dilated to one centimeter. I have a follow-up appointment in one week to check the baby's position. Thank you for Kate.

I never knew how to answer the question "How do you do it?" because I truly don't know. I didn't grow up hoping for five children—and certainly not for twins—but here I was at thirty-six years old with a six-year-old, a four-year-old, a twenty-month-old, and newborn twins. Mack and I had known I was carrying twins. Well, not at first, but we knew on December 12, 2012. Probably like you, I may not have remembered the significance of this date, but the two events coincided for me, so the memory blazes in my mind. Earlier that day, I had cried when I found out that our fourth baby was going to be twins. Later on the same morning, when news of the Sandy Hook shootings flashed onto the television, I cried again. I wept in disbelief that my husband and I were going to rear five children in this crazy world. I felt afraid. How would we protect them?

Allow me to change the topic and mention the best ever kid moment in an airport. My family were all standing in the baggage claim area after a wonderful trip, and Sam had graced us with an amazing poop. So I felt obligated to go ahead and change him quickly. We headed to the bathroom. I laid him down on the changing table, and he started screaming and writhing around. I picked him back up and looked at the changing table, making sure nothing was poking out. All was clear, so I laid him back down. He was screaming. He just didn't want his diaper changed. I was saying, "We are doing this, Sam. Sorry, bud. No one wants to smell that. … Almost done. Okay." He was still screaming, so I told him, "Bud, it's all over. Mommy doesn't want to listen to you scream, so come out when you're done screaming." I walked out of the bathroom and knelt down about five steps outside the door. The sweet janitor lady saw Sam coming and looked worried. I raised my hand as if to say, "Don't worry. He's with me." (Again I was claiming the screaming child.) Then Sam walked out of the bathroom and put on the best show of his life. His arms went straight down, his whole body got board-straight, and he let out the best gut-wrenching scream he could muster, red face and all. All the faces in the baggage claim looked at Sam and then at me. A woman came out of the bathroom looking very concerned. "Um, ma'am, ma'am, here is his pacifier. Do you know how scary this place must feel?" Now the woman was looking at me. "Have a heart. He's just a baby." I picked Sam up at this point. And all I could think was, *Well, he's not really a baby. This is a full-on toddler. And that, that was just a temper tantrum he threw for not getting his way, but okay.* The woman walked away, and then she came back. "I just want you to know I lost my only son at age twenty-six. And I would give anything to be able to hug him and tell him I love him. Just tell your son that you love him."

Oh, okay, that made way more sense. I said, "Thank you," meaning it, and then I smiled for the unsolicited correction of my mothering technique by a complete stranger. I understood where the woman was coming from, and I accepted her challenge to, at times, show a little more compassion to this little guy, toot or not.

After that, a beautiful woman walked up with her equally beautiful daughter and son, who must have been twins twelve or thirteen years of age, and their darling Lhasa apso puppy on a leash. They kind of looked like they had walked out of a movie. They were all so beautiful. The woman said to Sam, "This little guy [the puppy] was just telling me he needed a pat from you. What's your name? … Sam? That's a great name. Will you pet him? He really wants to feel better too." Sam loved it. He pet the little puppy. We both just stayed down, kneeling by this little puppy. I smiled with tears welling in my eyes and gave the woman a little nod as my thank-you. Grace from one mother to another: it's a healing balm for the soul.

I have now gotten used to answering the question "How do you do it?" And I've answered differently through the years. I usually say something like, "Oh, with help!"; "It's the hardest thing I've ever done"; or, more recently, "It's the most humbling thing I've ever done." Right? How else can you explain to someone what it feels like to be holding an infant with your two-year-old screaming and kicking at your feet in the middle of the most popular mall in Dallas? How else do you explain offering your children dinner each night while expecting the proverbial "Yuck!" to come out of their mouths? How else do you explain to the wedding planner with the beautiful engaged couple that your son had to go the bathroom ... in the middle of the arboretum? How else do you explain teaching your eighteen-month-old that if he can't find his pacifier in the middle of the night, then he is going to have to work it out—and then listening to him scream for two hours ("Oh, it will only be thirty minutes the first night, blah, blah")? How else do you explain walking into your three-old-son's room after calling him for lunch to find every article of clothing strewn on his floor and his completely naked body standing there as he wonders what to wear? How else do you explain finally trying to pee because your morning coffee has caught up with you, and you have a baby on your lap and two other faces staring back at you? How else do you explain taking the time in your workday to pump breast milk three times for the baby when you share an office with two colleagues? How else do you explain arriving at work with white diaper cream smeared on your collar and a puffed snack treat stuck to your rear ... and you hadn't even noticed? How else do you explain the half smile when you get asked again, "When are you due?", and your baby is a year old? Some mornings I would think, *I just want to sit for five minutes in silence with my coffee.* Hah, not today, Mama. Not this morning. Not today. It's why the most oversaid statement in all of eternity is "Enjoy every minute. Time goes by so fast!" Not today, lady, not today. Right? I'm just trying to keep my people alive. I'm not enjoying anything. I can't even sit with my coffee for one minute.

Do you remember what it feels like to enjoy a cup of coffee? I don't, because my life is not my own.

In many ways, I am *that* mom. Maybe you've even been her too. You know the one. She leaves her kid at school, doesn't bring the right lunch (whether in a throwaway container or a paper sack) on field trip day, and doesn't have the right sippy cup or the right pacifier for the certain child who needs it. I've left the stroller I needed, forgotten the Baby Björn (I know it's the Ergo now) when I had to have it, and failed to have a diaper when I *had* to have a diaper. And, you know, sometimes I just get tired of claiming the screaming, out-of-control child. Somehow it always feels like it's mine to claim, even when it's not my child. How is that possible?

Kate, my five-year-old, brought home a new friend for the first time. We went to the elementary school to pick up her big sister and then planned to head home to play. It was springtime. Lovely white dandelions were blooming, and there were bees, several, swarming about, so most people were avoiding a particular small area of patchy grass. I was having a conversation with another mom when I heard screaming that I did not recognize. And by now everyone within a hundred yards had turned around. It was Kate's sweet friend who was screaming. I am not even kidding. The bee had flown into her sandal and stung her twice on her foot. Awesome. That was a fun text to send to her mom: "Hey, just wanted to let you know that Lisa is fine, but she got stung by a bee. We put some medicine and ice on it. She says she wants to stay." I attached a picture of the happy child swinging. That was real. I was dying. We made it through. P.S. It was the first time that Lisa had ever gotten stung by a bee. I was thankful that I knew how to deal with allergic reactions.

Journal entry, September 17, 2011

I am weary this morning. I feel emotionally and physically drained. Who knew that four-year-old soccer could become a thing to dread and fear? Charley was typically worked up about her shin guards and then didn't want the green water bottle. Then she was upset because her team was playing on a different field. Then she needed her ponytail redone (the band broke when she was putting it back on, so I used mine). I got to sit with hair down my back, at thirty-seven weeks pregnant in ninety-five-degree heat. Joy. I talked to Charley about glorifying God in all she does. I walked her over to her team, and when I got back to my spot, she had run to the other field (which had no people on it) and was now yelling, "I am mad at my mommy!" over and over. Another sweet mom saw what was happening and went to help her. Then Charley got out on her own field. She was running and kicking the ball. Then she had to go the bathroom. Please remember, this is the third practice where we have had to go to the bathroom. There are no bathrooms and no Porta Potties, only trees. That's where we go. Except this time she got a strip of pee on the right side of her skirt (yes, skirt) and proceeded to emit ear-piercing screams at the top of her lungs. I looked up and saw a wall of parents and children who had, as if on cue, looked up with shocked faces. Charley sounded like she had been mortally wounded, but such was not the case. She took a breath or something, making the stares disappear, and then I asked her to go get her soccer ball and join up with her team. Instead she went running away from the field over to some tables with the same scream. Now moms were staring horrified.

All I could do was to say, "She's okay. She's actually okay." And then she proceeded to scream while walking five feet behind me, all the way across the fields and back to the car. Then she begged for a Kleenex.

Mama was leveled. As I sat at the coffee table with Kate on my lap and with tears streaming down my face, Charley came up to me and asked, "Mommy, are you sad? Why are you sad? Can I give you a hug so you will feel better?"

51

CHAPTER 5

Heels and Huggies

Journal entry, January 11, 2006

Lord, I sit in the living room looking at beautiful flowers—thirty cream, red, burgundy, and peach roses in a bud vase from my boss. And vibrant yellow Gerber daisies from sweet friends. What blessings! They glow like G. D. I miss him. He passed on January 4, and the funeral was January 9. What a man. What a servant. I've never known anyone like him. Such a servant. So selfless. So godly. So loving. When he was an eight-year-old boy, he played in his little league's championship game. In the ninth inning, his team was behind. He hit the ball into left field, ran to first base, and then ran to second base. The ump called him safe. "Hey, ump, I was out," he said. So the ump called him out. He lost the game for his team. I don't know who has that kind of character.

Samuel Jack. I give him to you, Father. I pray that he'll come into this world and love well. Lord, help me to love well like my grandfather. Help me to say kind words to people and about people.

I work outside of the home. I think this can be divisive issue number one in Christian circles today. Finally the SAHM (stay-at-home mom) and the "CEO" of the "fill-in-the-blank" family is getting much-deserved and long-awaited respect for the labor-intensive job of raising little ones. I have never done anything harder in all my life than to provide for, engage with, and lovingly discipline my little ones on a daily basis. I have a foot in both worlds (raising littles ones and the taking care of patients in an office), because my job allows me to work part-time. I see patients three days a week, which means I physically have to be at the office from 8:30 a.m. to 5:00 p.m., but not every day. On the other two days (and the weekends), I'm doing carpool, planning playdates, and hosting friends at our house. So I get it. And I tell people that my hardest day in the office is not as hard as a normal day at home with my kids. My patients ask me often, "How are you here? Who takes care of the kids?"

I've been tempted to use the line my counselor uses: "Oh, I just throw some Cheerios on the ground for them." I do not do that, by the way, just in case you were wondering. My children are in the very good care of a wonderful nanny. For me, working part-time has been my sanity. I was not sure when I was pregnant with my first child if I would be able to return to work. I called her the X factor. I had never had a baby before. Maybe I was not going to be able to leave her in someone else's care. I figured out that I could. I can tell you that I'm a better mom because of it. This is true for me, but it doesn't have to be true for you. Maybe you have to work full-time and don't feel like you have the choice and that feels hard. Maybe you work full-time, but your schedule lines up with your kids' and you have summers off, so it's a great fit. Maybe you are a SAHM and have a business that you do on the side working evenings, weekends, or whenever the kids are napping. Maybe you are a SAHM and wish you had a business that could be a creative outlet for you or just something to call your own. Let's not make it a spiritual issue. I mean, it is a spiritual issue, but it's one between you, the Lord, your husband, and the people you trust. I think we can get past the idea that staying at home full-time with your children is the only option or the most spiritual option. Right? (Come on, church—it's 2016.) Go be a light somewhere. Yes, be a light with your children, but you live in a neighborhood that needs hope. Are there children in your neighborhood who need to be loved? Will you invite them into your home, feed them, let them play, and show them what a family looks like? To me, that's work, especially when it's out of your comfort zone and maybe not your gifting. Open your doors. People need to know Jesus. My mom once asked me why I work. She had stayed at home full-time raising kids. I replied, "I work because the people I talk to actually listen. They may do what I recommend, and they get better." I enjoy the sense of productivity and of goals being reached, which is not the thing one gets on a daily basis with a toddler and a baby.

It was a chilly morning in January, but it felt very worth it to me to get the kids out and let them run and play. So my friend and I decided to meet at the arboretum for playtime and a picnic lunch. Her youngest is best friends with my second. I and my children were killing a little time before my friend came and discovered a beautiful waterfall we hadn't found before. There were beautiful big stones surrounding the waterfall and stone steps down to the pool below. And the pool was full of gorgeous orange and white koi fish. Kate (five years old at the time) and Sam (three years old at the time) were enthralled. Sam was climbing on the rocks, teetering precariously at times to get a better visual on the fish, so I didn't feel comfortable walking away from him knowing that he could plummet into the water in half a second. So my twins, Sarah and Crew, eighteen months of age, discovered that the sidewalk they were on actually went somewhere. Exerting a little independence, they ventured out. There was lush grass on either side of them and no trees, so I could see them well. Kate had just said, "Mommy, are we the only ones here?" It was a very quiet morning at the arboretum.

I was not concerned when I saw a woman walking behind a stroller with what looked like her mother by her side. She was a little ways off. As I looked again, I saw her arms go out to her sides in annoyance, as if she were asking, "What is this?"

I was thinking, *Are you kidding me?* And then, when she was five or six steps closer to me, she made the movement with her arms again. I was thinking, *Not today, lady, not today. You have no idea what my morning looked like. It took me two hours to clean up after breakfast, unload the dishwasher, and make a picnic lunch for four little ones and myself, because everyone at some point in the morning was crying—and several times they were all crying at the same time.* I looked this woman straight in the eye, pointed my index finger to the ground, and rather boldly said, "Are you kidding me?"

She responded, "Come take care of your kid."

I looked at her, put my arms out to the side, and said, "I am taking care of four, thanks."

In a very sarcastic tone, she responded, "Well, I hope he doesn't get run over by the stroller."

I answered, "I hope so too." I was simultaneously thinking, *You, lady, are an adult. You do have control over the stroller you are pushing. I am so sorry that you are so inconvenienced that you may have to slow down or step to the side.*

She says, "Oh, really? Oh, really? You hope he gets hit by the stroller?"

Aw, nah. *If I have to explain it to you, then it ain't worth it.* I kept my mouth shut. And guess what? Her mom turned around and said, "The sign says don't climb on the rocks." Silence. And then they walked away. I looked up and could not find sweet Sarah for thirty seconds. Count it up. It's a really long time when you can't see your child and you're dying inside on account of it. I could not see her. Kate ran all the way up the stone steps and came around the side, and my precious little Sarah-Beara was running out in front of her. Kate came up to me and said, "Mom, are you okay? Are you crying?"

I wiped my tears with the back of my hand. I said, "I'm okay, Kate. I'll be okay." I was still a little shaken when I found my friend and her daughter. We sat down for our picnic. An adorable mom, with her adorable girls, asked if she could join us for our picnic. We, of course, said yes.

Isn't it a glorious thing when you have a real sweet surprise connection with a person? I told the woman the story of what had just happened, and she replied, "What?! No way!" I felt validated, kind of like, *Okay, I may have just encountered a mommy bully.* That's the way it felt, anyway. I had never had that kind of interaction with another mom before. I mean, man, isn't being a mom hard enough? I feel like we're all in this together, like we're part of a sisterhood. Moms of little people, rise up! I think that when you have five children (and never thought you'd have five) and you have made almost every mistake in the book, there is a lot of grace coming from me. Do not hear me wrong. I am not perfect—far from it. I have received no awards, accolades, or five-dollar Starbucks gift cards for my mothering, only a sweet little hug or a sweet little card or a hand reaching up to hold mine. We mothers are all working really hard to love our children well so they can thrive. And sometimes that can be a very tricky balancing act.

I still remember when I heard about my friend A.B. (I will use her initials). I had just spoken with her sweet husband two days prior as we picked up our girls up from ballet. The couple were headed to Washington, DC, the next day for her brother's wedding. She hadn't told her OB about the trip. She wasn't due for another six weeks, but she and her husband knew what their OB would say. I had traveled on a plane three weeks before my due date with my second, so I naively said, "Oh, you guys will be fine. There are hospitals there too." And then the news came through: she had been in an automobile accident, a head-on collision. The baby was gone. She was alive, but the next twenty-four hours would be critical. I cried for four days. I couldn't stop. All I could think about was her lying in a hospital bed and fighting for her life, while we all prayed for her heart for when she would hear the news that sweet Charlie was gone. What prepares you for that moment when you wake up and you're alive and someone whispers, "The doctor said that if it hadn't been for the baby, you probably wouldn't have survived the impact." This sweet, precious life kept his mommy alive. Their middle daughter said, "Oh, Mommy, Charlie has always been an angel. He was always going to Jesus before us." To lose a child (I write in tears) is a grief I have not known.

A.B. is a fighter. She fought her way back through painful surgeries on her shoulder, elbow, hip, and ankle. Undergoing physical therapy has been her full-time job. Amid the craziness, she and I have gotten to sit while our daughters practiced ballet and, for about thirty minutes every week, had the opportunity to share. We laughed, we cried, and we talked about the Lord. And I was struck by how, by using such unique situations, the Lord was teaching us both similar lessons. We both were being stretched, pulled, and molded, and it was hard, humbling, and grounding. We talked about Jennie Allen and the IF: Gathering, about Ann Voskamp, and about how we were practicing gratitude one day at a time, one gift at a time. We talked about how under the circumstances, under the most gut-wrenching circumstances, we were choosing to say thanks. In the broken (both of us), in the loss (her), and in the overfull capacity (me), we were asking God to enter into it with us.

My prayer as a parent is that God will help me love my precious little ones to pieces and that they will know they are loved unconditionally.

To be loved but not known is comforting but superficial.
To be known and not loved is our greatest fear. But to be
fully known and truly loved is, well, a lot like being loved
by God. It is what we need more than anything.

Timothy Keller, from *The Meaning of Marriage*

I love my children when they are winning the race or falling flat on
their faces; when they are looking straight at me and hitting their brother
in the face for the ninth time; when I have asked them to stop doing that;
when they jump up and say, "Okay, Mom!" when it's time for dinner;
when my oldest (eight years old) says, "Mom, I do not have to always do
what you want me to do" as she walks into school for the day; or when she
says, "You're the best mom ever. Thanks for letting me have a playdate
with my friend."

The interesting thing about having five kids is that I do things that
I would have never considered doing otherwise. I have to calculate the
risk differently. Take the woman at the arboretum; that was a low-risk
situation. I was not worried; there was no problem. I was going to stand
by my son, who could have fallen into the water and drowned, because
that is far different from a twin tripping in the grass or getting in front of
another mother's stroller. With five kids, my threshold has to be higher. I
can't live getting worked up about the little things, or else I will *go crazy*.
So if my son is not listening or obeying, I may leave him where he is
standing (and/or crying) and come back to get him if I have another child
or two or three to drop off at the church nursery. If he decides to follow
me, perfect, but often he does not follow me because he's not ready to go
or because it wasn't his idea to go. It's a big church and there are security
guards. Again, it's a calculated risk. I wouldn't have done that if I had two
kids. I have done it since I have five.

And I do get annoyed with you, first-time mom (cringe), when you
are hovering over my shoulder as I pick up my kids. Many of us have been
there. I can feel your breath on my ear, because you're craning your neck
so hard to see what your child might be doing. Your child is fine. I have
two, so can you back off for just two seconds and let me get my children?
Then I will move out of your way. If something like this had happened

only once, I could laugh about it, but it happens to me every Sunday. I know, super-selfless me should just let her (or him!) go in front—and I have. I pick those babies up last now. The babies get picked up last because I'm more likely to run into someone who may be just slight more laid back, which makes all the difference. Oh, first-time mom, I was once you. I am you! I see your face, and I know you're fuming. Give it a year or two until child number two arrives. What you're doing now may make you laugh.

People make this type of comment a lot, but I distinctly remember when having two children felt very hard. Remember my lunatic toddler? Now I had a baby in the mix. It was not easy then either. So if you see my middle son crying while he's standing with his back against the wall (as I'm trying to drop off another child) and I see your worried face, raise my hand, look you in the eye, and say, "He's with me," but you continue to look worried, saying, "I just wanted to make sure he's not lost," will you just roll on? You have a tighter proverbial rope, and that's okay, but mine has to be longer. Don't' judge. It's just different for me, and it's okay. Do I really have to say, "Nope, he's not lost. I'm sorry that you are uncomfortable with the situation [he is only six steps away], but I have learned that this is what works best in this situation. He is a slow mover. And he does much better when he comes around and ends up thinking the whole thing was his idea to take his sister and then to be dropped off himself. I don't need you to act like I don't know what I'm doing just because it is different from what you may do"? We should not act like we know what it feels like to walk in another mother's shoes. We don't. We just don't.

We moms need each other. We really, really do. We need each other so we don't feel alone in the craziness. We need each other so we have someone to say the following to: "Oh, you too? I thought I was the only one." Whether these are real-life physical people in front of you or wonderful people you are connecting with through Facebook or Instagram—or whatever blog you may follow—it's beautiful when you connect.

> Straddling that yawning chasm between the parents we'd
> like to be and the parents we are, these moms and dads
> are, for me, a picture of how earnestly we want to be
> good parents, but how hard and humbling the experience

actually is. In the end, we all need a lot of grace. And this I find, is universal. All around the world, rich or poor, parents encounter their own weakness and their deepest vulnerability in their love for their children. We love so much and can control so little.[1]

Gary Haugen

I didn't grow up in the darling neighborhood I now live in, and I much prefer *real* conversations. Most people would say, "Yeah, me too. Who doesn't want to have real conversations?" Well, I have learned that people don't always like real conversations if they're about the hard stuff— the ugliness, the pain, the discontent, all of those parts of us we'd rather hide. I'm just not a good "how's the weather" type of friend, so I have a tendency to just be quiet. I take initiative with things but not with people. I'm a great responder (in friendships), but I do not excel at approaching new people or trying to make new friends. Maybe I fear rejection, or maybe I am simply afraid that people will not be as interested in going deep as I am, or that they may run scared when they learn about my "stuff." I'm not interested in yelling my stuff from the rooftops (um, not until now), because, well, we *can* be a judgmental lot, us moms, in an oh-so-subtle yet still judgmental kind of way. Reader, I have made every mistake in the book. My motherhood journey hasn't always been pretty, *but* I can own it and not wallow in the shame of it all. I have learned a lot through the years, and I know that I will continue to learn. The longer I journey on this road of motherhood, the more grace I have to give. Thank you, Lisa-Jo Baker and *Surprised by Motherhood*.[2]

Journal entry, June 2, 2013

And then came number three.

Samuel Jack,

We are so thankful for you and your precious life. You are a very loved son, grandson, brother, and nephew. You are named after two very important people. The first is

Samuel Evans, who is your great-grandfather. He died in 2006, before you were born. Mommy held his hand in his last days and said that her son would be named after him. He smiled at the thought. I also told him I would run a marathon for him. He ran several, most notably, the Boston Marathon when he was sixty years old. I ran the Marine Corps Marathon in Washington, DC, with his Shell Oil necklace around my neck. It was an honor. Maybe you will be a runner. I can't wait to see who you will become. Your maternal grandfather, Jack Lesch, was also a runner. He ran fifteen marathons total, with his most recent being in Oklahoma City in April 2007. Mommy and your aunt Jaclyn ran several miles with him. My prayer for you is that you will always run hard after Jesus, your mommy and daddy's Savior. I pray that you will come to know him as your own personal Savior and the author and perfecter of your faith. You are about to be a big brother of a brother and a sister! I couldn't love you more!

Love,
Mommy

CHAPTER 6

Beautiful Mess

One Thousand Gifts by Ann Voskamp changed my life. I don't want to be too dramatic by saying this. The change didn't happen overnight. Still, it was edifying to hear someone who feels as deeply as she, who wrestles as profoundly as she, and who can turn around and give thanks amid things that are hard, ugly, and ugly beautiful. I felt a kinship with Voskamp when she expressed her deep emotions. I liked her simile indicating that anger can be like a prowling lion. I felt like I had come to expect suffering, so I wasn't surprised when it came, but I was not in the practice of giving thanks for it until I read One Thousand Gifts.

At first, I just started breathing like Ann wrote about. I would breathe in whatever the moment held and then breathe out and say thanks. It sounds simple, but it is profound. I started doing this mostly in day-to-day life with my kids. Sam (three) was screaming about the sausage that I had just put on his plate. Seconds ago when he had asked for the sausage, he didn't mean it—and now this was all wrong. This is typical of the moments I knew would come, the moments when I want to run screaming from my home and just let someone else enter in. Are these the moments I'm supposed to give thanks for? I breathe out, saying, "Thank you, Lord, for the opportunity to love Sam, even during this moment. I invite you to take over, because my children are killing me."

Voskamp writes, "I look for the ugly beautiful, count it as grace, transfigure the mess into joy with thanks and eucharisteo leaves the paper, finds way to the eyes, the lips. Yes. Finds its way to the lips, so we are not whining or screaming in the hard, we are thanking. Eucharisteo always precedes the miracle."[1] I could not relate more.

Voskamp goes on to say, "I know it well after a day smattered with rowdiness and won a bit ragged with bickering, that I may feel disappointment and the despair may flood high, but to *give thanks* is an action and is a verb and these are not mere pulsing emotions. While I may not always feel joy, God asks me to give thanks in all things, because He knows that the *feeling* of joy begins in the *action* of thanksgiving."

The joy for me has come in the doing. My sister bought a beautiful journal from Anthropologie, one that is the perfect size for this endeavor (Rifle Paper Company, Botanicals Notebook Collection). In May of 2012 at my sister's bachelorette weekend in Sonoma, I started writing down the things I was thankful for: cool mornings, a good book to read, the mightiness of the Golden Gate Bridge, gruyère cheese, laughing until my sides hurt, giving surprise gifts, lingering over a cup of coffee, eating pasta with asparagus, sweet pea and mint pesto, soaking in a hot tub, throwing a spontaneous dance party, having an uninterrupted shower, and having enough hot water.

I am so good at this. (Laughter.) I would randomly write things down when I felt thankful. I filled up a few pages. I wrote several things down when the twins were close to arriving, and then I wrote a few things when they did arrive, including sour milk in the neck creases, Crew's contented milk moan, friends bringing meals, the night nanny (she stayed for four weeks; I cried a lot when she walked out my door for the last time), and the best blog post I've ever read on mothering the day the twins arrived.

Then the ugly beautiful came in October (when the twins were four months old): salsa spraying in my eye after it had dropped from the refrigerator to the floor; smoke in the house from an overmicrowaved taquito (my husband was the culprit; I hate the campfire smell); a sore throat; the overwhelming needs of five children; Sam's screaming; Kate's defiance; my plugged ducts and chubby belly; and mosquitoes.

And in 2014, I printed off the Joy Dare Collection every month and embraced the challenge of counting one thousand gifts. Each day was numbered and had three prompts, such as "three things orange"; "something wooden, wire, and mesh"; and "something wooly, soft, and woven." This journey of counting gifts wasn't perfect. I would sometimes do a whole week's worth—and sometimes two weeks' worth—at a time because I had forgotten to write each day. I didn't finish my entries for September and wrote nothing in October. I almost did the whole month of November, but I stopped after Thanksgiving and wrote nothing in December. So this year I'm going for it, start to finish. Nobody said it had to be perfect. I still have 921 gifts to look back on in 2014 and be thankful for them.

I felt challenged by Kara Tippetts' story of grace.[2] I cried when I heard she died. I cried while thinking of her sweet husband and four children who were missing her terribly. Then I smiled through the tears when I thought about her dancing in a new body in heaven. I loved what Ann Voskamp wrote about her. My favorite quote on the subject is, "Dying doesn't have to be a tragedy, if we avoided the tragedy of living for the wrong things." Then my mind quickly went to my sweet friend Jen, who has a similar story. She has metastatic breast cancer and just received news that the trial drug that she has been on while being treated at MD Anderson Cancer Center has stabilized the metastatic disease in her liver and bones, but her right breast (where the cancer started) has blown up like a water balloon. Jen and I were talking after church one Sunday. I gave her a hug. She said, "I think he's calling me home."

I nodded, looked up at her with a tear running down my cheek, and said, "I think so too, but I don't want you to go." And in the next moment, I looked over at my three-year-old son, who had pulled his shorts down to his ankles.

Jen said, "Oh yes, every day, these are my people!" I just laughed. And I let my son pee in the landscaping of the church. We attend a church with a congregation of ten thousand people. There were probably closer to three thousand at this service. The risk was that my son and I could trek all the way into the church building without my daughter knowing where we went. Also, my husband and oldest daughter were coming out to meet us and we would not have been there. Figuring that my son may not have made it to the bathroom anyway, I let him urinate there. There was a two-foot wall about five feet in front of him, and I protected him from the back. It took me half a second to process and eight long seconds for him to finish. See, I really have become that mom. It's about survival. I don't know how else to explain it.

Journal entry, February 16, 2014

John Piper at Watermark Church (via webcast, as I am home with Sam and the twins)

O Lord, forgive me, because I have been a Pharisee. I have compassion for others in their sin because I know I have received mercy. Much. But the older son was grumbling. He was with his father. His father entreated (not commanded) him, "I am with you, and all I have is yours." The son was grumbling because his father had it wrong. He did not love his father. He just wanted to be with his friends. I think I've just wanted to be anywhere but here, anywhere but in my life with the demands of five kids. I've even been doing my gratitude journal. Maybe it's not enough. Lord, forgive me. Forgive my grumbling spirit. Help me to dig in to you, to press in when I'm at the breaking point with nothing left to give. *Vaso.* That is Spanish for "empty." After Friday and throwing my guts up, that's how I feel: empty. I feel like the older brother in the story in the book of Luke. Piper said that that was the only time you were gentle with the Pharisees. At other times, you delivered harsh words. I am a Pharisee. I don't want to grumble, Father. You have given much. I have an overwhelming task. I can't do it without you. Help me to be thankful. Help me to find joy.

We have to fight for joy. We have to fight for joy so that we can experience freedom to go do what the Lord has called us to do.

PART 3

The Tension We Experience as Warriors

We build too many walls and not enough bridges.

Isaac Newton, from Latasha Morrison's Be The Bridge website

Deep within all of us there is a yearning to be brave. … When it comes to being brave we should picture the courage of Jesus—the power to fearlessly speak the truth, the freedom to selflessly love.[1]

CHAPTER 7

Warrior Women

"Perhaps you have been chosen *for such a time as this.*" This may be a familiar passage from the book of Esther. The entire verse is found in Esther 4:14: "For if you remain silent at this time, relief and deliverance will arise for the Jews from another place and you and your father's house will perish. And who knows whether you have not attained royalty for such a time as this?" Esther was in a critical place where she had the ear of the king to plead for her people and potentially save thousands of them from death. Her request of the king's presence put her life at risk. He could have said no, and then Esther would have perished. That is pretty crazy if you think about it. It's interesting for me to see this verse juxtaposed with 1 Timothy 2:12, which reads, "I do not permit a woman to teach or to exercise authority over a man; rather, she is to remain quiet." This is the verse that has silenced many women for generations. Now that sounds dramatic, but in many ways, the silencing of generations feels true at times. Maybe the verse doesn't mean that the woman is to remain quiet *all* the time. Maybe she should remain quiet when a teacher is teaching so that she can learn and be challenged. Maybe she should not be chatting or gossiping with her friends so as to disrupt others around her. Just like the case with the four gospels covering many of the same stories but each of them offering a different perspective, here we have two verses that are in seeming contradiction to one another. When should women not remain silent? Women have a tendency to want to lead. We do it well. And we can try to usurp power from men. And men can rule over women.

Maybe, just maybe, there is a time for women to speak out and to stand up. And maybe that time is now. If we do not, perhaps God will find someone else.

Jesus chose women. He spoke to the woman at the well and revealed to her who he was, the first time in recorded history he had done so. The most important news that the world has ever heard was of Jesus's resurrection, told to the world by women. The women were at the tomb at dawn and determined to spread the news (while the Twelve were in hiding). God used Rahab, who saved lives. Deborah was a judge and a warrior. Lydia was a savvy businesswoman. And the woman in Proverbs 31 was buying land, planting vineyards, and speaking well of her husband at the city gates.

How will we walk in what the Lord has for us today? Will we choose to go?

Esther didn't just go charging in. *Okay, I have a mission. I'm going in.* That's what I would have done: forward march. Instead, she asked for help. She said, "Mordecai, go tell all the Jews to fast and pray for me. For three days." She prayed and fasted too. "I and my maidens" will do the same, she said. "We will fast and pray for three days." Esther exercised humility. She went directly to the Lord. She chose to be with the Father. She pursued her mission humbly and boldly, a combination only possible by leaning in to the Father.

I recently read a collection of essays written in the 1830s and 1840s by black and white women who came together to fight slavery and racism. Known as the Abolitionist Sisterhood, they are credited with "forging the link between the abolition of slavery and the advocacy of women's rights which was to blossom in the Seneca Falls Convention of 1848."[1] These well-organized women met with increasing resistance. It got to the point that hostile mobs threatened their peaceful meetings. They defied the people who made the threats and increased their commitment to continue meeting. They issued this statement:

> We must meet together, to strengthen ourselves to discharge our duty as the mothers of the next generation— as the wives and sisters of this. We cannot descend to bandy (light) words with those who have no just sense of

their own duty or of ours, who dread lest the delicacies of the table should be neglected, who glory in the darning needle, and whose talk is of the distaff (woman's domain). This is a crisis which demands of us not only mint and anise and cumin, but also judgement, mercy and faith; and God being our helper, none of these shall be required in vain of our hands. Our sons shall not blush for those who bore them.[2]

I was in tears when I read that last sentence. *"Our sons (and daughters) shall not blush for those who bore them."* These women held this particular meeting on an October evening in the 1800s. When the masses found out where they were meeting, a crowd tried to break into the hall where the meeting was being held. These brave women still finished their order of business. One woman recounted what happened when they left the building: "When we emerged into the open daylight, there went up a roar of rage and contempt, which increased when they saw that we did not intend to separate, but walked in regular procession." Much of the anger was directed at the black members of the group, so the women "walk[ed] two by two, one black member linking arms with one white member, the white women offered protection to their black sisters, a form of nonviolent resistance which was to be used frequently by the female abolitionists."

Yes, I love this. Let's do this again. Let's link arms, sisters, and let's march together. Let's fight together against the injustices of the world. Because they are real. And we can't just stand by. The road will not be easy. There will be resistance. But if we face it together, we will become stronger.

Lucretia Mott "arranged for the women to go arm in arm, one black woman and one white woman. She herself led the column, and the women simply faced down the angry onlookers, relying on the moral force of their own courage and sense of right to protect them from attack. It worked. ... The women passed through the angry mob unharmed."

Margaret Hope Bacon went on to say, "The same faith in practical or applied Christianity which animated the early abolitionists to oppose slavery led them to believe that their fight for justice must rely solely on the weapons of truth and love."

It was the words of a woman that stirred the heart of William Wilberforce. Elizabeth Heyrick and several other women wrote a pamphlet in an effort to keep the sufferings of the slaves in the minds of the British people. They spoke the truth.

Mott went on to say, "I would be very glad if women generally and men too, could so lose sight of distinctions of sex and to act in public meetings on the enlightened and true ground of Christian equality." I feel this today.

She then said, "Because that was not yet possible, Mott felt there was 'perhaps no better or speedier mode of preparing them for this equality, than for those women whose eyes are blessed that they see to act in accordance with the light they have, and avail themselves of every opportunity offered them to mingle in discussion and take part with their brethren.'"

Amen. All I can think about is Ecclesiastes 1:9, which reads, "There is nothing new under the sun." Are things any different today?

Why does the message of the IF:Gathering resonate so much with me? Because it was women coming together regardless of age, race, or denomination and saying yes to Jesus. Absolutely beautiful! No one defined the way walking with Jesus should look for a woman or couching things a certain way so that they looked "right" in the context of Christianity. We came together to say, "Yes, that is the God that I believe in. I can pursue my dreams? Yes. Lord, you would have me go? Yes. Lord, I'm ready to go to the ends of the earth. Is that you want? Yes. Lord, you would use me? Yes. Do you need me where I am? Yes. Okay, I will stay. Lord, you are with me to walk in this journey that I would not choose? Are you helping me to be brave? Okay, I will go. Lord, show me what you would have me do."

We know God as our Father. We know about his power and might. We know him as ruler, protector, and provider. We know his strength and decisiveness. God has feminine characteristics as well. We should not be surprised about this. Genesis 1:27 tells us, "So God created man in His *own* image; in the image of God He created him; male and female He created them." He created human beings in his image, and his image was not complete without woman. This is a new concept for me. So God, as powerful and mighty as he is, cannot forget the baby at his breast. Isaiah 49:14–15 reads, "Can a mother forget the baby at her breast and have no compassion on the child she has borne? Though she may forget, I will not forget you!" God is saying this to Israel. Even as much as a mother may forget her child (not possible), he says, "I will not forget my people."

Who can relate to the mama bear analogy? In Hosea 13:8, God says, "I will meet them like a bear deprived of her cubs; I will tear open their rib cage, And there I will devour them like a lion. The wild beast shall tear them." Yep, sounds about right. God is saying that he is mad at Israel for withholding gratitude, so he is going to respond like a mama bear deprived of her cubs. He is saying, "I know what that feels like, to be wounded, to be in agonizing pain, and to have someone take my babies from me. I have been there." So God is not necessarily the gentle, merciful, quiet spirit that we associate as being more appropriately female.

The image of a lioness is another strong one. Proverbs 28:1 says, "The wicked flee though no one pursues, but the righteous are as bold as a lion." The righteous are as bold as a lion. Let's ask ourselves when the last time was that we were as bold as a lion. Again, the Lord is describing who the righteous are. This is who we are as men and women. Let's walk in it. Is it okay for a woman to be a lion(ess)? Some of us are. And it's the way God made us. Many have these characteristics even if they do not have a lion-based personality. They are direct and competitive; they are visionaries and decision makers; and they express their opinions readily.[3] A lioness can destroy a gazelle in order to have food (since she is actually the hunter) and then, with the same teeth, carry her cubs by the neck to safety. Another beautiful thing about lionesses is that, within the same pride, many will give birth at the same time so they all can help one another out. The lioness is a warrior.

The Lord goes on to say, "I know what it looks like to care for a child." Isaiah 66:12–13 reads, "For thus says the Lord: Behold, I will extend peace to her like a river, the glory of the Gentiles like a flowing stream. Then you shall feed; On her sides shall you be carried, And be dandled on her knees. As one whom his mother comforts, So I will comfort you; And you shall be comforted in Jerusalem." That is a very nurturing image. It is beautiful.

And then there is my favorite, Deuteronomy 32:11–12: "As an eagle stirs up its nest, Hovers over its young, Spreading out its wings, taking them up, Carrying them on its wings, So the Lord alone led him, And there was no foreign god with him." This is talking about how God led Jacob.

What is so interesting about this is the female imagery of a bird protecting her young. I did not know that female eagles are larger and stronger than their male counterparts. The female eagle is the main incubator of the eggs and the main hunter for the eaglets' ongoing sustenance. When it is time for the eaglets to leave the nest, she takes them on her wings and in one fail swoop she dives, letting them fly alone. She then recaptures them once they grow weak and weary. What a picture of what our heavenly Mother (I know, it sounds weird) does with us. We are so used to saying "heavenly Father," but this Scripture describes a motherly instinct. The image here is that of a mother. So, just as we are God's children and enjoy the protective covering that he provides, we are mothers, spiritual and physical alike, of children. And God gets it. He has placed a value on us. Does he want us loving our own children this way? Absolutely. Does he want us loving in the church? Absolutely, we are to be raising up the next generation. Does he want us loving in our places of work? Absolutely, we are to be a light. Does he want us loving on the global stage? Absolutely. It is as if God is saying to us, "Love my people and help them to fly on their own. Be gentle. Don't leave them, as they may grow weary until they have their strength. Love them as a mother would love her own. That's what I have done with you. Now, go and set my people free."

I will go ahead and mention here the beautiful irony in the fact that the United States of America has chosen the eagle for our national emblem. Probably one of our founding fathers was looking into the skies and saw a beautiful mother eagle hunting for food for her eaglets. She was chosen for her majesty and her limitless freedom amid the grandeur of nature. On our official seal, the eagle holds thirteen arrows in her left talon to represent the first thirteen colonies. In her other claw is an olive branch. She has her head turned to the right, showing her preference for peace. "Arrows in the hand of a mighty man, so are the children of youth. Happy is the man that hath his quiver full of them" (Psalm 127:4–5). The dichotomy of the arrows and the olive branch is meant to indicate that we seek peace but are always ready for war.

I love the image. It is of a mother eagle pondering her mission. "Until they [her children] learned how to soar, they would fail to understand the privilege it was to have been born an eagle."[4] When eaglets are separated from their mother at birth, they never learn to fly. They walk around on the ground like chickens. They may even look up at some other eaglets and think, *Oh, wow, they look like me and they are flying.* Eagles have to be taught how to fly, and it is the mother's job to teach them. And do you know what she does first? Just as verse 11 says, "She stirs up the nest." She literally begins to take the nest apart. She takes out the soft cushion of the leaves and heaves them over the cliff. Then she begins to remove the framework, the key branches that make up the nest. She knows that the eaglets will never learn to fly if they stay in the nest. And neither will we. This is why the term *empty nest* exists. I would say that the Lord is saying, "Well done, Mama. You did it. You taught your children how to soar. Watch and be amazed." That's what he wants for all of us, to soar. He wants us to walk in our God-given place, whether we are we teaching, singing to an audience, mothering, or running a company.

CHAPTER 8

Taking Up Arms Together

I can tell you one thing—if Jesus had the opportunity
to actually lead His Church, women would be powerful.
Jesus refused to let the religious leaders of His day oppress
women. It is about time that we become Christlike in this
area today. [1]

Kris Vallotton

I have been waiting to hear someone say what you've just read above.
The Bible does not support the idea that women are subservient or
of a lesser design. First Corinthians 14:34–35 reads, "The women are to
keep silent in the churches; for they are not permitted to speak, but are
to subject themselves, just as the Law also says. If they desire to learn
anything, let them ask their own husbands at home; for it is improper for a
woman to speak in church." The context for this passage is this: during the
time when Paul wrote it, women and men did not sit together in church.
At times, a woman would ask her husband a question during the service,
thereby disrupting others. In this day and age, we would not say that this
directive should still be promoted. We do not think that women should
literally not speak in church. So why do we hold so strongly to 1 Timothy
2:12–14, which reads, "I do not allow a woman to teach or exercise
authority over a man"? Paul was writing to Timothy, who was teaching to
a community in Corinth that was highly influenced by Artemis, a goddess.
He struggled because the Corinthian people often elevated females above

males. Paul was saying, essentially, "Do not let this be." Some authors say that a better translation is that a woman should not teach with the purpose to dominate over a man. Right, that's different than stating that a woman should not teach a man. So now the question is, what is at the heart of what you are doing? There are other interesting facts to consider when dissecting this verse, such as the word *diakonon* (which appears in the original Greek), which can mean "servant, deacon, or minister." Phoebe is listed as a "servant" of the church (Romans 16:1). She was likely an official church deacon. The exact same word, *diakonon,* is almost always translated as "deacon" or "minister" when used to describe a man. Let's go back to the Word of God to see what it says about women, but let's not make it say something it doesn't say.

> The truth is that the absence of the feminine and matriarchal presence in leadership has come at an incalculable and sometimes cataclysmic expense to society. ... We do not need women to lead like men. The world is starving for matriarchs who are compassion driven, intuitively gifted, nurturing leaders. These leaders foster the maternal instinct in society that gives birth to a much more loving, caring, patient and compassionate planet. It is my honest conviction that if women were commissioned to lead in their rightful place and role globally, the planet would be a much safer, more compassionate, nurturing place to live. Violence and war would dramatically decrease worldwide if women would co-lead with men, without feeling the pressure to lead as men.[1]

That men and women are equals is indisputable if you look at the Bible. Now that the debate on complementarianism versus egalitarianism, which I am told has been wholly divisive, has lasted for many years and has drawn no conclusions, it can end. The Enemy must love it. This is an issue that has kept hundreds of bright minds focused on minutiae that are irrelevant and has kept God's people from their kingdom work. I am going to say it right here and right now: it's over. We'll just decide. It's not even a thing anymore. Done. And for those of us with boots on the ground, those of us who have been walking with the Lord for, oh, I don't know, thirty, forty, or fifty years, it never was a thing. Please, come. Come out of your silos and get your feet dirty.

In 2 Samuel 20:16, Joab, the general of an army under the command of King David, was summoned by an unnamed wise woman. She wanted to meet with him. He went. Joab was on mission to kill Sheba, who had risen up against the king, and in his endeavor he began to destroy the city where Sheba was hiding. The wise woman wanted to find a solution without destroying her city, which was the "mother of Israel." She approached Joab humbly, calling herself his servant. She spoke boldly, and she did not let her emotions rule. Instead of freaking out over the fact that her home was about to be destroyed, she bravely found a solution. She asked, "Why are you doing this to our city?" Joab replied, "I just want one man, Sheba." She responded, "His head will be thrown to you from the wall." That was bold. She had the ear of her people (who in turn agreed with the plan) and of the commander of an army. Who was this wise woman? She came humbly and boldly and was in a place to know God's call on her life when she heard it, because she had been regularly spending time with him. And she walked in what she was called to do. That's one warrior woman I would like to be.

God's kingdom work is going to happen.

My sister, Sarah Bessey, wrote the following:

Women are preaching already.

I hate to break it to you. Women have always preached, just as women have always worked, always taught, always discipled, always followed Jesus. Right from the days of Jesus until now.

We're [women] getting on with it [kingdom work]. We kept walking from the statement to the question to the answer and now we are living within the freedom of Christ.

Jesus is working through and in and with women, just as he is working through and in and with men. And wouldn't you know it? Women and men are working together, beautifully, in what Carolyn Custis James has christened the "blessed alliance." It's not either-or, it's both-and.

We are made in the image of God, watch us walk on water together.

Men and women are receiving steady and sober, wild and holy teaching from women, too. People are being healed, the Spirit is baptizing many. Women are leading in the curve of the globe in business, medicine, technology, academics, sports, and yes, religion in ways unique to their temperament and anointings.[2]

Could we agree that there just may be something to this Blessed Alliance? And maybe, just maybe, it is actually God's design. One man plus one woman equals one glorious servant. It is a concept similar to the Trinity. The math doesn't add up, right? One Father, one Son, and one Spirit equals one God. What does it mean? He needs all of us. The work cannot be complete without women. The work, the way God envisioned it to be, cannot reach its glorious potential without women doing what God designed for us to do. He wants for all of us to use our God-given gifts and serve. The Blessed Alliance is the "rich, collaborative, interdependent relationships between God's sons and daughters vital to both genders to make the body of Christ stronger. The Blessed Alliance fuels the kingdom of God and must not be displaced by an atmosphere of tension, fear and mistrust."[3] The only way that works is for people to serve sacrificially—for men and women to serve sacrificially. Another great line from James's book is, "A lot of people believe the earth will spin off its axis and civilized culture will collapse if men do not maintain their authority over women in the church and the home. Jesus doesn't share that fear."[3] It should be reassuring for those who may have this concern to know that Jesus is not worried about that. Because you know what? The people—dare I say, the large majority of them are men—who may still have this fear are making the issue become one that is about them instead of about the Father. Jesus's vision was that his image-bearers would be as one. "May they be brought to complete unity to let the world know that you sent me and have loved them even as you have loved me" (John 17:23). The world will not know Christ unless we are capable of serving sacrificially—each one of us, male and female alike, together. So that may mean that men must make space for women to serve alongside them. And it may mean that women must step into that space, because it is where God has them. This Blessed Alliance is going to happen with or without us. Let's do this.

I learned some things about myself when I was working through *Restless,* a book designed to help the reader discover different threads in her life in order to be able to move forward in the work of the Lord's kingdom. I fight uncertainty. I am uncertain about the Lord's will. I am uncertain about writing this book.

In her book, Jennie Allen writes, "He is in the trenches with us. In the fear. In the uncertainty. He is in the unknown—knowing and leading and working. What we don't know yet is meant to lead us to dependence."[4] And that is exactly where God wants us to be—on our knees, desperately dependent on him. And he can be very creative about how he gets us there. For me, it's been the needs of five small children (abundance) and a hard marriage (grief). Each of us has our own story about how he has gotten us there. Often it is *not* in neon lights. It is a simple act, word, or question that he lays on our heart and that we can't shake. What I learned about myself in looking at moments at different life stages and discovering why I'd felt satisfied was that I fear achieving something outside my comfort zone. As I think through my next steps for the future, I feel like He is asking me to step out of my comfort zone again. One of my passions is helping people as a Physician Assistant, not only treating their medical conditions but also listening to what they say about what is in their hearts. Another passion is loving and investing in my children. I have a new brewing passion for justice for women. My eyes were opened recently to the fact that African American women are three times more likely than Caucasian women to have a preterm birth, the single most important reason for infant mortality (infant death in the first year of life after a live birth). Medical science has no idea why this is so, but not for lack of trying. Researchers are looking, but no threads are emerging. To me, it is not that large of a leap to consider the state of American culture as it stands today and how it may be impacting people. Socioeconomic status, racism, the dissolution of the family—is it any wonder? Racism is still alive and well in our country, and it is sickening. Generation Xers and millennials have no excuse for being racist. God's children, our sisters, are wearing the scars of generations of cruelty.

It's about equality, about women on the same playing field as men. We are not just cheering from the stands; we are playing. I'm not saying women are better than men. This is not a bra burning, but this *is* black women on the same playing field as white men (gasp) and Hispanic men on the same playing field as Caucasian men. We're all at the table. This world needs all of us, including those of us willing to lead. *Lead on in the name of Jesus.* Lead. Love. If there is going to be change in this world, then it will take all of us to make it happen—women and men of all colors, all of us. This is *not* about women rising up against men. This is about women joining up *with* men. I have grown up as a white woman in middle America, with arguably every opportunity at my fingerprints. If I have felt held back by paternalistic hands, how much more must my sisters in other countries and my sisters with different colored skin? May it not be. May it never be. My heart is drawn to my sisters, all of my sisters who may have felt this in many different ways and to different degrees.

We are made in God's image. We are his children. He sees us. He wants us to soar. It will take extending grace to other believers (who may be doing things differently than we are; come on, ladies!) and extending kindness to those who do not know Jesus. There is lots of kindness in the world, and people giving to others. Consider Red Nose Day. I think sometimes it's harder to be kind in our habitual places, for example, at a retail store with the worker who will not give us cash for our return, with the fast food attendant who messes up our order or takes a very long time, in the carpool line at our kids' school. Oh, showing kindness in the carpool line. We all need Jesus for that.

The most beautiful picture I have seen here on earth of what heaven may look like is a Sunday morning service at All Soul's Church, Langham Place, in London, England. It is an historic building full of beautiful people from places around the world—India, Africa, and Turkey, just to name a few. At twenty years old, I had never seen anything like it. John

Stott, who wrote *Basic Christianity* and was a leader in the evangelical movement, pastored this church from 1950 to 1975. I met him in 1997 and had tea in his flat. I wish my thirty-eight-year-old self could go back. I'd probably have a few different questions for Stott, like, what is the most effective way to help the marginalized, a way that also allows the helpers to love them well?

When I read *The Locust Effect* by Gary Haugen, I cried while reading Yuri's story of rape and murder in Peru.[5] A seven-year-old girl was raped and then murdered at a family party. There were witnesses who saw two men, brothers, leaving the home where it had happened late at night. Those same men had the means to find the best lawyer in town, who literally covered up the evidence. The bloodied mattress was scrubbed clean and resewn to half its size to remove the incriminating section. Vaginal swabs of the girl's body were taken in the family's home while the family gathered to grieve her death, because the original swabs had been lost. The same lawyer presented himself to the girl's family saying he was there to help them. While there, he scooped up the last remaining evidence, her clothing from that night. I've been to Latin America and seen the people's faces, their smiles, and their tears. Then I wanted to yell at the book, "Don't give your baby's bloody pants to the other lawyer. He's not trying to help you!" And in fact, he wasn't. It was only a gross underhanded abuse of power to squash the evidence. The girl's mom has spent her life savings to pay other lawyers to seek justice. Those lawyers take her money and do nothing. I wept at the injustice in the world.

What is also shocking is that the International Justice Mission (IJM) has a presence in many of these countries in order to stop slavery and human trafficking. The IJM's agents have been shocked at the functioning judicial bodies and law enforcement agencies in many countries. What they have discovered is that many countries are still functioning under archaic colonial law, which is designed to protect the powerful elite, not the poor. Police officers are not trained, and have no incentive, to protect the poor. The systems are designed to make it virtually impossible for a poor person to bring a grievance against anyone in a position of authority. There is no doubt that law enforcement and a functioning public justice system must be in order to bring justice and deter violent predators.

All I can think about is the other part of the story: the social causes of violence, including gender bias, marginalization of vulnerable groups, lack of education, etc. As I sat in an introductory-level health behavior class, I was blown away by the implications of something called moral disengagement. Interestingly, as the professor introduced the social cognitive theory, he brushed over the moral disengagement as a random part of the theory that didn't seem to fit. Knowing about IJM and their work, I had this moment of, "We've got to get out of our silos and start talking to each other." That's more of an academic joke, but there is some truth to the image of everybody working in their own space but never talking to one another to find out how we could be working together. That's still a longing of my heart.

So, yes, law enforcement has to be, but how do you regulate for moral disengagement?

Albert Bandura's social cognitive theory (SCT) is very important in health behavior research. He is most famous for the concept of self-efficacy, which is one's confidence in his or her ability to perform behaviors that bring desired outcomes. Self-efficacy has been repeatedly validated and is important in health behavior outcomes, which is the whole point of research (to identify if the intervention actually works or helps people). Self-efficacy has proven to be very important in people's starting a positive health behavior or stopping a negative health behavior. Behavior can be changed by increasing self-efficacy, thereby increasing confidence. An increase in self-efficacy can be achieved through "new learning experiences, guidance in the adjustment of perceptions, and support the development of capacities."[6]

Bandura labels mechanisms of moral disengagement, which include euphemistic labeling, dehumanization and attribution of blame, diffusion and displacement of responsibility, and perceived moral justification. What does all of that mean? Its sounds pretty heady, but some of these are things we all do every day. Euphemistic labeling can include things like using the term *friendly fire* to describe a soldier's being shot by one of his own comrades; *adult entertainment* to describe pornography; *enhanced interrogation* when speaking about torture; *family planning* in place of "contraceptives"; or *feminine protection* to indicate tampons. One example from the US government is its changing the executive Department of War to the Department of Defense in 1949. The two are the same thing.

Dehumanization and attribution of blame indicates perceiving targets (who become victims) as ethnically different and at fault for their punishment. I would use the Rwandan genocide as an example. In Jacqueline Murekatete's *100 Days of Genocide*, she writes, "On a daily basis, radio broadcasts called us 'inyenzi' or cockroaches, inciting our Hutu neighbors to start killing us."[7]According to Bandura, the process of dehumanization is an essential ingredient of the perpetration of inhumanities. And we keep seeing inhumanities today. ISIS is on the move and gathering jihadists. Wanting the Ottoman Empire to be resurrected, they are currently taking over land to make this possible. Christians are the bad guys, and we are being targeted.

Diffusion and displacement of responsibility is made possible by attributing decisions to a group or to authority figures. The tobacco companies have mastered this art from their decades of tobacco marketing, which has sought to display an image of who we want to be (or whom we want to be with, e.g., the Marlboro man). They justify beliefs about personal freedoms in their effort to continue promoting a known cause of cancer. Diffusion of responsibility also goes with a group mentality, which assumes that everyone is responsible so that no one person is to blame. This has been studied. It has been shown that people act more punitively under a group-responsibility mentality than under an individual-responsibility mentality.

Stanley Milgram has done research that has been widely cited because it unearths the shocking reality of how easy it is to bring out the worst in people through dehumanization, which—can we be honest right here?—must be why people say the craziest, meanest, ugliest things on social media. I think we should set up an experiment like the one Jimmy Kimmel has been doing, but in ours, the "mean person" has to sit there while the person reads the mean tweet, post, or comment. What is interesting is the opposite effect, which is that most people will not behave cruelly, even under authoritative command, when the situation is personalized by their inflicting pain directly and watching the suffering caused. Bandura says, "The emphasis on obedient aggression is understandable considering the prevalence of people's inhumanities to one another. But the power of humanization to counteract cruel conduct also has considerable social import. People's recognition of the social linkage of their lives and their vested interest in each other's welfare help to support actions that instill them with a sense of community. The affirmation of common humanity can bring out the best in others."[8]

Social cognitive theory describes how people can learn moral standards for self-regulation, which can lead them to avoid committing violence against and being cruel to others. I wish it were that easy.

CHAPTER 9

Weary Warriors

God will bring us to our knees, whatever it takes to get us there. Whatever it takes for us to daily and desperately depend on him, He will do. So if life feels easy or comfortable, be thankful. As a result, He might have something for you. There are sweet, happy moments in life, no doubt, and they are a gift, but those moments for me occur in the midst of suffering. As an independent mom who likes to have the answer for everything, I am on my knees every day, because I cannot raise five children in my own strength. I can't. I tried and I ended up on Lexapro 20 mg. Now, it's Lexapro and Jesus. For now, I am completely comfortable availing myself to modern medicine. I'm not going to hide that fact. I don't even feel like I need to or should. Right now, I need the medicine, and I do not feel that it is weak of me to say that. I do not think that I am going to need the Lexapro forever, but right now I do. I do not feel like the fact that I take a selective serotonin reuptake inhibitor discredits me or takes away from my story. It is part of my story. These days, I say yes to help when it is offered. I have to ask for help from others. I have to say "I don't know" a lot. I hate it, but I'm learning how to do it. I'm learning how to accept this place. I'm learning how to find the balance between asking for help and offering to help. For example, I have children over for playdates a lot. I have not always felt comfortable with this. I felt like it needed to be the perfect situation in order to invite my kids' friends over, "perfect" meaning that I have a clean house, I am well rested, and I found the perfect craft on Pinterest and have all the supplies to make it! I can even laugh at myself now. What's funny is that as my children get older, they need me to take the lead less and are happy to come up with their own fun. Hallelujah! I can be okay in the craziness, because there is grace. *But what if I need medicine?*

I wrote the following e-mail to my pastor:

Dear Tim*,

Thanks for all you do, and thanks for always challenging your flock to be fully devoted followers of Christ.

I have been at our church for fifteen years, and I thought I'd send my first e-mail on an issue that I feel pretty strongly about. I would respectfully ask that you speak cautiously when sending the message from the pulpit that antidepressants are somehow "bad" or "not okay." I attended the first service Sunday morning, and the comments surrounding "pills in a bottle" sought in isolation seemed to disregard the very real fact that oftentimes people are taking antidepressants (and may have even made that decision with their community), in a community group, attending women's Bible study, and actively serving. Antidepressants (including counseling) and living in community / being a fully devoted follower of Christ are not mutually exclusive.

I understand where you are coming from, and I understand that you see people who are living in isolation, but for those of us who are not, there is nothing wrong with availing oneself of modern medicine. It's kind of like treating diabetes. Type 1 diabetics are low on insulin, so they inject insulin into their body to live. When your body is low on serotonin, sometimes, for a season, you need a boost in your serotonin stores, so you take an antidepressant. And nobody needs to feel guilty or judged for making that decision. For me, when I am taking care of my children (who are seven, five, three, and twenty-one months old [this last being the age of my twins]), I need a higher threshold to love them well and to discipline them lovingly. One day, I hope not to have to take an antidepressant, but my circumstances haven't changed, so for today my family benefits from the 20 mg of Lexapro that I take daily.

The response that I received from my pastor's assistant was that I should watch a recording of a talk that he had given at a conference in Dallas. I listened to all fifty minutes of his talk on despair. The message that I got was to identify sin in my own life, read the Bible every day, and cling to Jesus. In my typical (former) fashion, I thought, *Yep, that's great. Can't argue with that. Identify sin, read the Word of God, and turn to Jesus.* Then I kept thinking about it. Then I panicked. I felt that if this is the message that the church is giving, then *people are going to die.* If the church is going to subtly say that antidepressants are in fact not okay in any situation, then people are going to *die.* I was doing those three things my pastor advised people to do in his talk. I wasn't doing them perfectly, but I had just finished up a yearlong study on Genesis; I was serving in a ministry at my church for sexual abuse survivors, facing my own sin and the sin that had been done to me; and I had never journaled more in my life (that's how I cling to Jesus). My skin was crawling, and I was waking up in the middle of the night with a heaviness in my chest that I had never felt before.

What do we do when those three suggestions are not enough? What do we do when Jesus is not enough? I hear myself asking the question, and I am like, *Can I even ask that question?* I'm gonna go ahead and ask it. Now, hear me out. If I could live in a home, sit with my Bible every day, drink coffee in the morning, and go on a run every afternoon, then Jesus would be enough. The antidepressants that I take don't make my children disappear. The children, all five of them, are still there with their relentless needs. And my hard marriage is still there too. I have never had to expend more of myself more consistently than I do with my children. And I get to see my failures up close every hour. Every mother understands this. And I don't feel like I'm accomplishing anything, so for an achiever, I feel like a failure. And I'm an introvert. Truthfully, I'm always in the middle, between introvert and extrovert, but my tank gets filled up when I'm alone. Insert the laughing-with-tears emoticon. I'm never alone. Or at least it feels that way most of the time. And sometimes that's all I want, to go and be alone. Antidepressants don't magically propel me into some alternative universe; they just allow me to have a higher threshold for my people.

Note that antidepressant medication won't make you better all by itself. If there is sin in your life that you aren't willing to look at it or face, then you should gain the courage to face it. If you aren't in the Word regularly, then go for it, as it can be a lifeline. And hold onto Jesus when it feels like he is taking everything away. The pills won't fix whatever the problem is, but let me say right here, as one representative of the church, that antidepressants are okay. They have to be okay, or else we are going to lose out on the gifts and purposes of fellow sojourners. We are going to lose people to their battle with depression or despair, whichever word you want to use. Our church community just lost one of those beautiful sojourners. Maybe I'm weird, but I will choose people taking a medication for their illness in order to remain in this battle we call life.

And on that note, I will go on to say that counseling is a beautiful thing, just as living in community with others is a beautiful thing. These things do not have to be mutually exclusive. I agree with Jennie Allen when she states, "Everyone should have a counselor."[1] Exactly. Especially people who don't think they need a counselor should have one. Just sayin'. Preach it, sister. Why not? For me, counselors enabled me to make huge strides in seeing things about myself that I would not have been able to see otherwise. And my community was thankful that I went to counseling, because my husband and I had exhausted their energy and capabilities. They loved us well in our turmoil, conflict, and chaos. They did exactly what a trustworthy community does. They came alongside us. At some point, a couple can't dominate the time or else it begins not to feel like community. Because of my counselor, I dug into the pain of the sexual abuse that I thought I had long ago "gotten over." The truth was that I had not gotten over it. The effects of it were affecting my marriage and my children. I was not connecting the dots, not seeing that my abuse twenty years ago was the reason that I felt betrayed by my husband (for even small things) and the reason that I felt like such a failure when outings with my high-demand, high-energy, highly sensitive first child did not end happily. My community and friends were very happy to listen and very happy for me to have advice from an expert. Now, woe to you who is going to a counselor to get fixed, never intending to tell another soul, and staying in a ministry position that would be best filled by someone else. Don't hide. God's wrath is far more terrifying than anything humankind can bring as we face the consequences of our own actions.

I recently sat with my friend whose husband is in ministry. She said, "I feel like the Lord is moving, like he is going to do something big with women. But I'm nervous, because we could miss it if we're not humble." And this theme keeps popping up over and over. If women are humble, then we can hear the "voice" of the Lord. In other words, we can hear the Spirit impressing things on our heart. If we are going to blow through barriers and decide that we are just going to lay hold of what we think is rightfully ours, then it will not end well. It will look ugly. I know that it is only with the Lord's help that I can do "nothing out of selfish ambition or vain conceit, but with humility of mind regard one another as more important than yourselves, do not merely look out for your own personal interests, but also for the interests of others."[2]

We could miss it. Let's not miss what the Lord is doing, ladies. Let's be watching and listening for his cue to release us to *go*.

CHAPTER 10

Eshet Chayil (Women of Valor)

I think that Ann Voskamp is on to something huge: *The Joy Dare. One Thousand Gifts.* She stated that a person could be "25% happier" by practicing gratitude. After learning this, I had to look up Michael E. McCullough who had actually proven this point through years of research. He has done many studies, including "The Grateful Disposition: A Conceptual and Empirical Topography" and "Counting Blessings versus Burdens: An Experimental Investigation of Gratitude and Subjective Well-Being in Daily Life." Gratitude has been described as the parent of all virtues. And I think in many ways it is just that.

The first study that McCullough et al. worked on looked at which personality traits and emotional states were associated with gratitude. The first study looked at the personality traits measured against the Gratitude Questionnaire–6 (GQ-6). Measures of well-being (life satisfaction, vitality, subjective happiness, optimism, hope, and psychological symptoms [anxiety and depression]) had the strongest correlation with gratitude (sometimes greater than 0.5, meaning that feelings of well-being are 50 percent or more the reason for gratitude. If it were exactly 1, then it would mean that feelings of well-being accounted for 100 percent of your gratitude. To put it another way, if you have feelings of well-being, then they would always lead to gratitude). There is also something called the Big Five Inventory (Big Five), which entails forty-four brief descriptive phrases that are markers for five personality areas: agreeableness, conscientiousness, extroversion, neuroticism, and openness. McCullough also found that agreeableness had the strongest correlation with gratitude

(0.39), while neuroticism had the strongest negative effect at −0.30. McCullough et al. did a second study on a bigger population (more than twelve hundred participants) who were mostly adult women (80 percent). These women, probably a similar population to those who are reading these words, were contacted via the Internet. The results were the same. A third study showed similar results, with envy and materialism being included. The researchers found that materialism and envy had strong negative correlations to the measures of gratitude.[1] Interestingly, what they concluded was that "material success was not a very important factor to highly grateful people." I love that.

The second study, "Counting Blessings versus Burdens," had some interesting conclusions as well.

In the first study, subjects were asked to complete a weekly gratitude journal, a weekly burdens journal, or a weekly neutral journal for nine weeks.

> Gratitude Condition: There are many things in our lives, both large and small, that we might be grateful about. Think back over the past week and write down on the lines below up to five things in your life that you are grateful or thankful for.

> Burdens Condition: Hassles are irritants—things that annoy or bother you. They occur in various domains of life, including relationships, work, school, housing, finances, health, and so forth. Think back over today and, on the lines below, list up to five hassles that occurred in your life.

The grateful group showed increased well-being, slept better, and exercised more. I'm in! They felt like life was better (8 percent) and had increased optimism (5 percent).[2]

In the second study, subjects were asked to complete a daily gratitude journal, a daily burdens journal, or a downward social comparisons journal for only two weeks.

> Downward Social Comparison Condition: It is human
> nature to compare ourselves to others. We may be better
> off than others in some ways, and less fortunate than
> other people in other ways. Think about ways in which
> you are better off than others, things that you have that
> they don't, and write these down.

In the second study, perhaps because the duration was only two weeks (versus nine for the first study), no significant impact of the gratitude intervention was noted on health variables (sleep quality, hours of sleep, alcohol usage, caffeine usage). Those in the gratitude group did report prosocial behavior (helping with a problem and providing emotional support for others).

I also find it interesting that gratitude is described as an affective trait: a built-in personality-level trait that determines how often and deeply we feel gratitude. All I can think is that I'm in trouble. A lot of us, those of us who do not have the built-in personality trait, are in trouble.

"An Adaptation for Altruism? The Social Causes, Social Effects, and Social Evolution of Gratitude"[3] found that gratitude evolved as a mechanism of reciprocal altruism. Reciprocal altruism is a social interaction phenomenon where an individual makes sacrifices for another individual in expectation of similar treatment in the future. The most interesting piece of supporting evidence is that we feel significantly more gratitude in response to the acts of strangers than in response to the acts of family members. As altruism by its nature is meant to help strangers, not those with whom we share DNA, gratitude excludes family members. This is disheartening, because it suggests that experiencing gratitude for family members on a regular basis requires fighting our biology.

Fighting our biology or fighting our flesh—it's really the same thing. I feel like I do that every day. I have a tendency to feel that my husband owes me, that he's obligated to help me. After all, they are his kids, too. So, we have to be intentional about noticing the little things and saying thank you.

That's what this means for me: saying thank you and being grateful for the little things. I wonder what happens to all those numbers and all those outcomes when we fight our biology and choose to be grateful for the burdens, the hard stuff, the pain, the ugly beautiful. What happens when we say thank you for the sexual abuse, for the severe mercy of the DUI, for the hard marriage, for the desperate needs of five kids, for the barren womb, for the broken friendship, for the loss of a child, for the disabled child, for the loneliness, for the infidelity, for the job loss, for the discrimination, for the promotion that should have been ours, for the husband in jail, for the wayward child?

How do we have or find gratitude for the good, the bad, and the ugly? I was interested as I read through the four methods for increasing self-efficacy in my *Health Behavior* textbook. I read about mastery experience (the strongest influence of the four), which enables a person to succeed in the attainable but increasingly challenging performance of desired behaviors. Next comes social modeling—showing a person that others like him or her can do the behavior. Social modeling should include detailed demonstrations of the small steps taken in order to attain a complex objective. The third method is improving physical and emotional states—making sure people are well rested and relaxed before attempting a new behavior. This one made me laugh, because nobody will ever be ready to attempt a new behavior if they have to wait around for that. The fourth method is verbal persuasion—telling a person that he or she can do the particular behavior (or stop a particular negative behavior), providing strong encouragement to boost confidence enough to induce the first efforts toward behavior change. Yes, yes, we need all of that!

I think joy is something that we fight for, something that goes against our natural biology. We learn how to appreciate the hard things daily. Every day there are three things that we can be thankful for. Some of the things I am thankful for are as follows:

- Grace from people I love
- Charley's excitement about eating fish
- Sam sharing his toy fire truck with Crew
- Having an after-school snack date with Kate
- The sunrise as our 4-man exercise group finished Max 30
- Sarah with sunglasses on
- Crew lying out on the ground and crying when I left for work

- Lots of patients
- A very sick patient

So, we should seek daily to identify at least three things that we have to be thankful for, which sometimes includes the ugly beautiful. I like the idea of thinking through events or circumstances that may never have happened, being grateful for an outcome that was uncertain at the beginning, or being grateful for an experience that may soon be ending. What would be the effect of writing in a gratitude journal for a whole year? What would be the effect of increasing our gratitude? What about the effects of forgiveness? What effect would letting go of anger and bitterness have on us? Would there be a cumulative effect?

A study titled "Positive Psychology Progress"[4] found that instructing participants to write down three things that went well and the causes every night for one week had a long-lasting impact. After one week, participants were 2 percent happier than before, but in follow-up tests, their happiness kept on increasing, from 5 percent at one month to 9 percent at six months. All this happened even though they were only instructed to journal for one week. Participants enjoyed the exercise so much that they just kept on doing it on their own. What could that mean for us if we just kept being thankful and continued daily to name in our journal three things we were grateful for? Could it mean that we would be grateful for where we were, which would lead us to more readily step out of our comfort zone? Could it mean that we would hear what the Lord was asking us to do more clearly? Could it mean that we would move in a way that would allow us to give a blessing and not expect anything in return (kind of like reciprocal altruism, but without the reciprocal)? Could it mean that the Lord would move us to a place where we were not sure we wanted to go? Could it mean that we would move to a place of forgiveness?

In my little homogenous community I am trying to step out. My community is so small that it is almost not even worth mentioning, but you know that God can use the small things too. It was a very subtle prompting in my heart to obey what the Lord was asking me to do. I was taking my oldest daughter to her talent show practice. I parked my car behind another woman's car. She said, "Oh, I'm so sorry. Is this your house?"

I replied, "No, I'm just doing the same thing you are—dropping my daughter off for practice." She leaned in to her backseat and pulled out this teeny, tiny baby. I asked, "Can I walk your daughter up to practice for you?"

She answered, "Oh yes, thank you. That would be such a big help." So I did. It was very simple. And then I felt like the Lord wanted me to offer to do this for the remainder of the time. So, I sought out the same woman after practice and said, "I would love to take your daughter and bring her home from practice for the next several weeks. I know you don't know me, so maybe that's weird, but I am happy to help."

She said, "Thank you so much. That would be great."

This experience opened up good conversations with my daughter, who asked me, "Mom, are these apartments for people with dark skin?"

"No, Char, they are for everybody."

"Well, it looks like they are for dark-skinned people, because that's all I see."

"Well, anybody can live here, but what is good is that this is a place to live, but it's not as big as a house. So, for A's mom, she can live here with her children and be safe. I'm not sure where A's daddy is. A can live here with her brothers and sisters and go to your school. And that's good."

"Okay."

And now a bigger step of faith. A Be the Bridge group launching in just days. Thank you, Latasha Morrison for inspiring us all to be bridge builders in our places whether work, home or church. One of the goals of this movement is to build a community of people who share a common goal of creating healthy dialogue about race.

I have a dream featuring you, featuring us: warrior women going where no man (pun unintended) has gone before, like to the moon, for those of you too young to have even seen this in your history book. The moon was once uncharted territory, scary, uninviting, and at the very least, unknown. Literally, no one had set foot there. So let's go there. Where is that for you? Where is the uncharted territory to which the Lord is asking you to go? Is it time to ask for a promotion? Is it time for you to start your own thing, you know, that thing you've been dreaming about? Is it time for you to ask that mom over for a cup of coffee—you know, that mom who isn't easy to love? Yes, that one. Is it time to show her kindness

94

because you have been given much and now you see it? Is it time for you to just do the gratitude journal? Ask three of your tennis friends and start today. Select a prize for whoever does it every day for six months, and then keep going! Is it time for you to push that little (not so little) one from your nest? Is it time to set some boundaries with a friend or with your husband? Is it time for you to go back to school for that degree? Is it time to go pursue a doctoral degree and show that gratitude has physical health implications for mamas and their babies, and that health outcomes can be changed? Oh, wait, that one is mine. Is it time to stop living in isolation and to tell your community about that thing you could never tell them before? Is it time to go to marriage counseling? Is it time to get on medication for depression? Is it time to start a reading/tutoring program for children at your child's school or a sister school? Is it time for you to go serve in another country or start a girls' school in Afghanistan? Is it time for you to knock on your neighbor's door and introduce yourself? Is it time to take more than a few seconds with that acquaintance to ask how he or she is *really* doing?

Do I think that Jesus is enough? I do. We must all think so. But we have to fight for that differently than a man does. And we will. When you walk in those dark places, the places that you never thought you'd go, Jesus is there with you. He has gone before you. In that room where my abuse happened, I believe that the Lord was there. He was weeping with me. His heart was grieved as I suffered, but he knew that it would be for my good. He knew that I would have but a glimpse of what other sisters have suffered. He knew that I would marry a man who did not know how to validate me so that I would return to the Lord and say, "I'm enough, because you have said that I am. You chose me. You chose us." He knew that I was going to have five children and be leveled because I could not raise them in my own strength. For now, with help, I am walking forward, moving toward what God has for me. And I do have tension—tension as a woman, as a working mom, and as a warrior. That arrow would not fly if there were not tension in that bow. The bow is pulled taut. If there were not tension or inner striving in my soul, in our souls, then things would just stay the same. Jesus has us here for a reason, just like Esther, for such a time as this. What king will you face today? What brave step will you take in order to walk in what the Lord is showing (or has shown) you? The time is now. Wherever you are, whatever you do, look at the people next to you. Acknowledge them, and then step out toward them. The Lord needs all of us in our place so we can walk in what he has for us, however small or big. Let the Lord use the tension that you feel, because it's real and it's there. The unrest is his tugging at your heart. You will be stretched. Watch what happens. Pull back on that bow. Keep pulling. You can do it. Watch the arrow fly and maybe even soar.

> Be merciful to me, my God,
>> for my enemies are in hot pursuit;
>> all day long they press their attack.
> My adversaries pursue me all day long;
>> in their pride many are attacking me.
> When I am afraid, I put my trust in you.
> In God, whose word I praise—
> in God I trust; *I will not be afraid.*
>> What can mere mortals do to me?
> All day long they twist my words;
>> all their schemes are for my ruin.
> They conspire, they lurk,
>> they watch my steps,
>> hoping to take my life.
> Because of their wickedness do not let them escape;
>> in your anger, God, bring the nations down.
> Record my misery;
>> list my tears on your scroll
>> are they not in your record?
> Then *my enemies will turn back*
>> *when I call for help.*
>> By this I will know that *God is for me.*
> In God, whose word I praise,
>> in the Lord, whose word I praise—
> in God I trust; *I will not be afraid.*
>> What can man do to me?
> I am under vows to you, my God;
>> I will present my thank offerings to you.

For you have delivered me from death
and my feet from stumbling,
that *I may walk before God*
in the light of life.

Psalm 56

Let's walk on sister warrior into the light of life without fear. He is for you.

Discussion Questions

Chapter 1

1. Where have your places of suffering been? Are you in one now? What are you learning from it?

2. Are you a survivor of sexual abuse or know someone who is? The statistics indicate that 25 percent of the women reading this book have been sexually abused. It's a big deal. The shame is not yours to own. Don't waste any more time minimizing the abuse.

3. In what ways are you hanging out in the "middle ground"? Where has God asked you to step out?

Chapter 2

1. How are you believing the best of your husband? Is this easy for you to do, or do you have to work at it?

2. Which part of WENI can you own? How can you do better in that area (or those areas)?

3. What was it about your husband that you fell in love with? Is that still the best thing about him? Are there new things that you have discovered about him?

4. What are your favorite things to do together as a married couple? (Do you have examples that don't include the kids?)

Chapter 3

1. What about the God gulf? How can we build a bridge? Have you tried to do this? Did it work or not?

2. How have you loved someone well who believed differently than you? How could you love well in the future?

3. Have you experienced racism in your life? If not, have you witnessed someone else being a target of racism? Did you defend that person? Why or why not?

Chapter 4
1. What is on your "should do / should not do" list?
2. What is your response to "Being God's Man" and "Being God's Woman"? Do you agree with the two lists? Why or why not?
3. What is your most humiliating mom moment that someone else witnessed? Please share. What is your most humiliating mom moment that someone else did *not* witness (screech)? Please share.

Chapter 5
1. Who has inspired you to take new ground in your mothering journey?
2. How have you judged other moms? How can you extend grace to them?
3. Is there anyone specific you should seek forgiveness from?

Chapter 6
1. How do you fight for joy? Does it help you in the trenches with your kids?
2. Are you able to say thank you for the hard, the ugly beautiful?
3. How are you different with others, or how do you want to be different with your kids, friends, or others (in this fight for joy)?

Chapter 7
1. What has the Lord used in your life to bring you to your knees?
2. Do you believe that we could actually see greater things than what Jesus saw in his lifetime?
3. Which analogy (eagle, bear, or lioness) do you relate most to?

Chapter 8
1. What is your understanding of what the Bible says about women?
2. What are your thoughts on the Blessed Alliance? Have you seen this in action or been a part of it? Have you experienced the opposite?

3. How can you take a step toward racial unity/reconciliation in your neighborhood, in your workplace, or at your children's school?

Chapter 9
1. Have you struggled, or are you struggling, with depression or despair? How did you struggle well? How did you not?
2. Do you feel free to talk about your struggle with other women? Why or why not?
3. Did medicine and/or counseling serve as a helpful part of your healing?

Chapter 10
1. Is Jesus enough for you?
2. Warrior woman, where would the Lord have you go?
3. Where have you gone?

References

Epigraph

[1] Shauna Niequist, *Bittersweet: Thoughts on Change, Grace, and Learning the Hard Way* (Grand Rapids: Zondervan Publishing, 2013).

Introduction

[1] *Merriam-Webster.com*, s.v. "tension," http://www. merriam-webster.com/dictionary/tension.

Part 1: The Tension We Experience as Women
Chapter 1: Facing the Darkness

[1] Cynthia Kubetin and James Mallory, *Shelter from the Storm: Hope for Survivors of Sexual Abuse* (Burbank: McGee Publishing, 1994).

[2] Nichole Nordeman, vocal performance of "Brave," by Paul K. Joyce, recorded May 24, 2005, on *Brave* (Sparrow, CD).

Chapter 2: Head Over Heels

[1] S. Stanley, D. Trathen, M. Bryan, and S. McCain, *A Lasting Promise: A Christian Guide to Fighting for Your Marriage* (San Francisco: Jossey-Bass, 2008).

Chapter 3: Embracing Our Differences

[1] US Department of Justice, Civil Rights Division, March 4, 2015, *Investigation of the Ferguson Police Department*, March 4, 2015, accessed March 29, 2016, http://www.justice.gov/sites/default/files/opa/press-releases/attachments/2015/03/04/ferguson_police_department_report.pdf, 68–70.

[2] Maria Dixon Hall, "A Teachable Moment: How OU Failed Transformation 101," *Patheos.com*, March 10, 2015.

[3] Michelle Alexander, *The New Jim Crow: Mass Incarceration in the Age of Colorblindness* (New York: the New Press, 2012).

4   Debbie McDaniel, Forty Inspiring Quotes from Elisabeth
    Elliot, accessed May 17, 2016, http://www.crosswalk.com/faith/
    spiritual-life/40-inspiring-quotes-from-elisabeth-elliot.html.
5   Sarah Bessey, *Jesus Feminist: An Invitation to Revisit the Bible's
    View of Women* (Brentwood, TN: Howard Books, 2013).
6   Nicholas Kristof and Sheryl WuDunn, *Half the Sky: Turning Oppression
    into Opportunity for Women Worldwide* (New York: Vintage Books, 2010).
7   Katie Davis, *Kisses from Katie: A Story of Relentless Love and
    Redemption* (Brentwood, TN: Howard Books, 2011).

Part 2: The Tension We Experience while Working (as Moms)
1   Tina Fey, *Bossypants* (New York: Reagan Arthur Books, 2011).

Chapter 4: The Demanding "Should Do" List
1   Personal communication.
2   Ruth Simmons, "Parenting in Weakness," *Gracelaced*, June 16, 2013, http://
    www.gracelaced.com/blog/2013/06/16/parenting-in-weakness.
3   Sally Clarkson, *Mission of Motherhood: Touching Your Child's Heart
    for Eternity* (Colorado Springs: Waterbrook Press, 2003).
4   Elaine Aron, *The Highly Sensitive Child: Helping Our Children Thrive
    When the World Overwhelms Them* (New York: Harmony, 2002).

Chapter 5: Heels and Huggies
1   Gary Haugen, *Just Courage: God's Great Expedition for the Restless
    Christian* (Downers Grove, IL: Intervarsity Press, 2008).
2   Lisa-Jo Baker, *Surprised by Motherhood: Everything I Never Expected About
    Being a Mom* (Carol Stream, IL: Tyndale House Publishers, 2014).

Chapter 6: Beautiful Mess
1   Ann Voskamp, *One Thousand Gifts: A Dare to Live Fully Right
    Where You Are* (Grand Rapids: Zondervan, 2011).
2   Kara Tippets, *The Hardest Peace: Experiencing Grace in the Midst
    of Life's Hard* (Colorado Springs: David C. Cook, 2014).

Part 3: The Tension We Experience as Warriors
1   Gary Haugen, *Just Courage: God's Great Expedition for the Restless
    Christian* (Downers Grove, IL: Intervarsity Press, 2008).

Chapter 7: Warrior Women

[1] J. F. Yellin and J. C. Van Horne, *The Abolitionist Sisterhood: Women's Political Culture in Antebellum America* (Ithaca: Cornell University Press, 1994).

[2] Ibid.

[3] Gary Smalley, *Personality Interpretations*, Smalley Institute. http://smalley.cc/images/Personality-Test.pdf. Accessed May 17, 2016.

[4] S.M. Paul Khurana and Paul Singhal, *Higher Education: Quality and Management* (New Delhi: Gyan Publishing House, 2010).

Chapter 8: Taking Up Arms Together

[1] Kris Vallotton, *Fashioned to Reign: Empowering Women to Fulfill Their Divine Destiny* (Minneapolis: Chosen, 2013).

[2] Sarah Bessey, "Why Not Have a Woman Preach," *Sarah Bessey,* May 11, 2015, http://sarahbessey.com/why-not-have-a-woman-preach/.

[3] Carolyn C Custis James, *Half the Church: Recapturing God's Global Vision for Women* (Grand Rapids: Zondervan, 2015).

[4] Jennie Allen, *Restless: Because You Were Made for More,* (Nashville: Thomas Nelson, 2014).

[5] Gary Haugen, *The Locust Effect: Why the End of Poverty Requires the End of Violence* (New York: Oxford University Press, 2015).

[6] K. Glanz, B. K. Rimer, and K. Viswanath, eds., *Health Behavior and Health Education: Theory, Research and Practice,* 4th edition (San Francisco: Jossey-Bass, 2008), 176–80.

[7] Jacqueline Murekatete, Rwanda 15 years later: A Survivor's Reflections, The World Post, May 17, 2016, http://www.huffingtonpost.com/jacqueline-murekatete/rwanda-15-years-later-a-s_b_185271.html.

[8] Albert Bandura, Moral Disengagement: In The Perpetration Of Inhumanities, *Personality and Social Pyschology Review* 3 (1999): 193-209.

Chapter 9: Weary Warriors

[1] Jennie Allen, "Why (I Think) Everyone Should Have a Counselor," *Jennie Allen,* May 19, 2015, http://www.jennieallen.com/why-i-think-everyone-should-have-a-counselor/.

[2] Philippians 2:3-4

Chapter 10: Eshet Chayil (Women of Valor)

[1] Robert A. Emmons and Michael E. McCullough, "Counting Blessings versus Burdens: An Experimental Investigation of Gratitude and Subjective Well-Being in Daily Life," *Journal of Personality and Social Psychology* 84 (2003): 377–89. Accessed March 29, 2016, doi: http://dx.doi.org/10.1037/0022-3514.84.2.377.

2   Michael E. McCullough, Robert A. Emmons, and Jo-Ann Tsang, "The Grateful Disposition: A Conceptual and Empirical Topography," *Journal of Personality and Social Psychology* 82 (2002): 112–27. http://dx.doi.org/10.1037/0022-3514.82.1.112.

3   Michael E. McCullough, M. Kimeldorf, and A. Cohen, "An Adaptation for Altruism: The Social Causes, Social Effects, and Social Evolution of Gratitude," *Current Directions in Psychological Science* 17 (2008): 281–85.

4   Martin E. P. Seligman, Tracy A. Steen, Nansook Park, and Christopher Peterson, "Positive Psychology Progress: Empirical Validation of Interventions," *American Psychologist* 60 (2005): 410–21. http://dx.doi.org/10.1037/0003-066X.60.5.410.

CPSIA information can be obtained
at www.ICGtesting.com
Printed in the USA
BVHW030831120321
602395BV00020B/68